EPHESIANS

Joyce Meyer's Biblical Study Series

Ephesians
James
Galatians
Colossians

EPHESIANS

A Biblical Study by

JOYCE MEYER

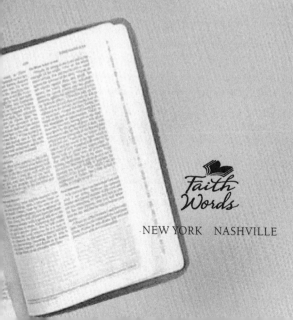

Faith
Words

NEW YORK   NASHVILLE

FaithWords
Hachette Book Group
1290 Avenue of the Americas, New York, NY 10104

faithwords.com

twitter.com/faithwords

First published in hardcover and ebook in March 2019.
First Trade Paperback Edition: January 2020

FaithWords is a division of Hachette Book Group, Inc. The FaithWords name and logo are trademarks of Hachette Book Group, Inc.

The publisher is not responsible for websites (or their content) that are not owned by the publisher.

The Hachette Speakers Bureau provides a wide range of authors for speaking events. To find out more, go to www.hachettespeakersbureau.com or call (866) 376-6591.

Library of Congress Cataloging-in-Publication Data has been applied for.

ISBNs: 978-1-5460-2602-0 (trade paperback), 978-1-5460-2600-6 (ebook)

Printed in the United States of America

LSC-C

10 9 8 7 6 5 4 3 2 1

CONTENTS

ABOUT EPHESIANS

Author: *Paul*
Date: *About AD 60*
Audience: *Christians in the city of Ephesus and in nearby churches*

Paul's letter to the Ephesians is a well-loved book of the Bible that teaches believers some of the most important lessons of our faith, such as who we are in Christ, how we are to live as followers of Jesus, and how to gain victory in the spiritual battles we face.

Paul probably wrote this Epistle as a circular letter, which was addressed to the Christians in Ephesus but was also meant to be shared with surrounding churches.

Ephesus was a large, influential commercial city in modern-day Turkey. According to bibleandhistory.com, "In the New Testament era it was the fourth greatest city in the world." Spiritually, this cosmopolitan city was the center of worship for the goddess Artemis. It was full of occult practices such as sorcery, astrology, fortune-telling, and perversion, including prostitution in the temple. Against this backdrop, we can understand why the Christians in Ephesus needed the strong teaching and encouragement Paul provided in this letter.

Most likely, Paul wrote Ephesians about AD 60, during his two-year imprisonment in Rome. I have visited the prison where Paul was incarcerated, and I could see that his circumstances there must have been extremely hard. History tells us that the city sewer ran nearby, so we can assume that not only was the prison dark and uncomfortable, but it also smelled bad. In the midst of such hardships, Paul chose not to focus on the daily difficulties of his life but on helping other people by writing to his fellow believers to encourage them in their walk with God.

Before we even begin looking at the text of Ephesians, we learn an important lesson as we think about Paul's circumstances when he wrote it: no matter how difficult your life may be during certain seasons, remember to do all you can do to bless, help, and encourage others.

The entire letter of Ephesians is six chapters. Chapters 1–3 are about who we are in Christ, the amazing things Jesus has done for us, how much He loves us, and our relationship with God, and chapters 4–6 are about how we are to behave as Christians. This sequence is very interesting because it reflects exactly what we should experience in our walk with God: first we become established in our personal relationship with God, and then we learn to grow in holiness—changing our thoughts, words, and actions so we will think, speak, and act as God would have us think, speak, and act.

No matter how much we love God, when we read the first three chapters of Ephesians, we can't help falling more and more deeply in love with Him. When that happens, changing our thoughts, words, and behavior becomes not something we feel we have to do to get God to love us, but something we want to do because we begin to see how much He loves us and we love Him so much in return.

A lot of people have misunderstood how to make changes in their thinking or behavior. They have tried to change based on their human strength or willpower and they have failed, ending up disappointed and frustrated. Ephesians teaches us that we absolutely cannot change by simply trying or through self-effort. We cannot change because we are motivated by fear that God will not love us if we don't. The right motive for changing is to want to please God as a way of expressing our love for Him in response to His amazing love for us.

One of the most vital and refreshing lessons of Ephesians is that relationship with God must come first. That's the key to effecting change in your life. If you will take time to develop a strong relationship with God, begin to see how much He loves you, and know who you are in Christ, change will come, and out of that relationship your life will bear the good fruit that God intends.

Key Truths in Ephesians

- Being "in Christ" is a spiritual reality, the most important spiritual reality in which you can live.
- In Christ, you are unconditionally loved and accepted.
- You are saved through faith, and faith alone—not through anything you can do.
- In Christ, you have victory in the spiritual war.

CHAPTER 1

—◆—

A SOLID FOUNDATION

God's Will

Ephesians 1:1

Paul, an apostle (special messenger, personally chosen
representative) of Christ Jesus (the Messiah, the Anointed),
by the will of God [that is, by His purpose and choice],
to the saints (God's people) who are at Ephesus and are
faithful and loyal and steadfast in Christ Jesus:

A building cannot be built properly unless it is constructed on
a solid foundation, and our Christian lives cannot be properly
built to withstand the storms of life unless we have a solid
foundation. Ephesians 1 is about the foundation of our walk
with God. In it, Paul discusses several things that are of great
importance to those who are children of God.

First, Paul clearly establishes that he is an apostle *by the will*
of God. He did not call himself to the task of being an apostle.
Whatever we do in life only works well if it is God's will for
us to do it. Too often we decide what we want to do and then
pray for God to make it succeed, but our relationship with God
doesn't operate that way. His will must be first in all things.

Being in God's will always produces peace in our lives, so
checking to see if we have peace in a situation is one primary way
we can discern whether or not what we are doing is indeed His
will. Also, when we are following God's will, what we are doing

works well. We may face opposition and times when we need to press through difficulties, but ultimately God's will always produces peace and good fruit. It is not God's intention for us to struggle through life, but we will unless we are in His will.

The first step to being in God's will is to want His will with all your heart. Pray that God will keep you in the center of His will, and if you are aware of anything in your life that needs to change in order for that to happen, then ask the Lord to help you make the necessary adjustments. If you truly want God's will, He will guide you and help you know what to do.

Personal Reflection

As far as you know, are you in the center of God's will at this time in your life? If not, what can you change in order to be able to say yes to this question?

_____

_____

_____

_____

_____

_____

_____

_____

Grace and Peace

Ephesians 1:2

Grace to you and peace [inner calm and spiritual well-being] from God our Father and the Lord Jesus Christ.

Paul didn't begin his letter to the Ephesians with "Hello, how are you?" He greets the people by saying, "Grace to you and peace." He used this greeting in several of his letters to the churches, and if we understand it properly we will see that it is very powerful. Paul wanted the people to enjoy a peaceful life, but he knew they could only do so if they understood God's grace and knew how to receive it.

We can think about what grace is in two ways. First, grace is God's undeserved favor, and we all need that on a daily basis. Second, grace is God's ability and power to help us do whatever we need to do in life. It can make impossible things possible and difficult things easy. I like to define grace this way: grace is God's undeserved favor and His power that enables us to do with ease what we could never do on our own with any amount of struggle or self-effort.

Are you enjoying a life filled with peace? If not, it may be because you have not yet learned the importance of living by God's grace. Our salvation comes by grace through faith in Christ (Eph. 2:8), and "by grace" is also the way we must learn to live our daily lives if we want to have peace. Jesus clearly said that apart from Him we can do nothing (John 15:5), yet most of us try to do some things for a long time before we finally surrender our fleshly efforts and learn how to receive grace (God's power and ability) for everything we do.

For many years I was frustrated, and I struggled with trying to change myself, to change others, and to change circumstances that I now realize only God could change; therefore, I had no peace. The more I have learned to live by grace, the more I have enjoyed peace.

Personal Reflection

On a scale of 1 to 10, with 1 being the lowest and 10 being the highest, how much peace do you regularly enjoy? What could you change in your life that would increase your peace?

_____

_____

_____

_____

_____

_____

_____

_____

Spiritual Blessings

Ephesians 1:3

Blessed and worthy of praise be the God and Father of our Lord Jesus Christ, who has blessed us with every spiritual blessing in the heavenly realms in Christ.

This amazing verse tells us that we have already been blessed with the spiritual blessings that are available from God. Spiritual blessings are different than material blessings. A person may have great material wealth and be at the top rung of the ladder of worldly success, yet be bankrupt when it comes to spiritual blessings such as salvation, peace, joy, satisfaction, contentment, being in right relationship with God, wisdom, and true spiritual power.

God has provided everything we need, yet we often waste years of our lives trying to obtain things that mean much less than what is already ours from God. These spiritual blessings are ours as a child of God. They are our present possessions, but we have to ask: have we possessed our possessions? What I mean by that is that no matter what God has provided for us, His gifts don't help us unless we receive them by faith. We receive by faith through believing the promises of God. For example, God has promised us wisdom and joy. Do you believe that you have wisdom? Do you believe that joy is already residing in your spirit, or are you trying to find joy in things that have no ability to ever give you true joy?

I have a house, and it has a lot of great stuff in it. I also have a key to my house, which gives me access to all of the stuff inside. But if I don't use the key, then the things inside the house do me no good. The key to all the good things (spiritual blessings) God has already provided is a belief that they belong to us. We can live with a childlike faith that simply accepts what God says without needing physical proof. Faith is the proof of the things we hope for and the evidence of their reality (Heb. 11:1).

The more we realize what God has already done for us through Jesus and the more we receive those things by faith, the more we are able to truly enjoy life. Our real life is not found in our circumstances, but in us. Jesus said that the Kingdom of God is within us (Luke 17:21). This means that we will never access spiritual blessings and the things of God by looking to external surroundings or resources; we will find them in our hearts.

Try getting up each morning and thinking, *I have everything in me that I need to have a wonderful day because God has already blessed me with every spiritual blessing that is available in the heavenly realm.* You will find this kind of thinking to be much better than trying all day to find something to make you happy and then being disappointed at the end of each day because somehow what you thought you wanted evaded you once more.

Personal Reflection

What do you think you need to have in order to truly enjoy your life? Have you possessed the possessions God has given to you?

_____

_____

_____

_____

_____

_____

Loved, Chosen, Adopted, and Accepted
Ephesians 1:4–6

Just as [in His love] He chose us in Christ [actually selected us for Himself as His own] before the foundation of the world, so that we would be holy [that is, consecrated, set apart for Him, purpose-driven] and blameless in His sight. In love He predestined and lovingly planned for us to be adopted to Himself as [His own] children through Jesus Christ, in accordance with the kind intention and good pleasure of His will—to the praise of His glorious grace and favor, which He so freely bestowed on us in the Beloved [His Son, Jesus Christ].

Everybody wants to be chosen. Do you remember being a child waiting to be chosen for the dance team, the cheerleading squad, or a sports team? I do, and the fear of not being chosen, which meant being rejected, was agonizing. Perhaps you were not chosen for the sports team, the promotion at work, or the worship team at church, but God wants you to know that He has chosen you. Anyone who believes in Him will never be rejected. Knowing we are chosen by God gives us confidence to live life boldly and without fear.

We often hear the terms *election* and *predestination* in connection with these verses. This is simple to understand if we look at it properly.

God planned for our salvation and redemption from the foundation of the world. He knew that man would sin, but God is never without a plan and a remedy suitable to fix any problem. He planned in the fullness of time to send Jesus His only Son to pay for our sins. We cannot take any credit for our salvation. God planned, Jesus paid, and our part is merely to believe and receive.

Someone asked a little boy if he had found Jesus. He answered, "I didn't know He was lost, but I was, and He found me." Again and again believers are spoken of as the chosen of God. Let this reality sink into your soul: *you are chosen!* God wants you. He accepts you. He has adopted you.

God's Word teaches us that even if our mothers and fathers have rejected us God will take us up and adopt us as His own children (Ps. 27:10). This verse has been very comforting to me because my natural parents did not love me as they should have. Their rejection left me with a wounded soul and with dysfunctional behavior, but knowing that God chose me, adopted me, and loves me unconditionally has brought healing and wholeness to me. That same healing is available to anyone who will receive it.

In addition to choosing us, God also predetermined that He would love us. Before you or I ever arrived on planet Earth, God had already decided that He loves us with a perfect and unconditional love. We do not have to earn God's love; He gives it as a free gift.

Has God chosen some people and not others? Absolutely not! His grace is available to all, but sadly, some will refuse to receive it. H. A. Ironside told this little story in his expository commentary on Ephesians:

> When asked to explain the doctrine of election a brother once said, "Well, it's this way, the Lord done voted for my salvation; the Devil done voted for my damnation; and I done voted with the Lord, and so we got the majority" (H. A. Ironside, *Ephesians: An Ironside Expository Commentary* [Grand Rapids, MI: Kregel Publications, 1937; repr. 2007], 19).

God has already voted, and all we need to do is vote with Him. It is God's will that all people should be saved and come to know the truth (1 Tim. 2:4).

Just as all of us desire to be chosen, we also crave to know that we are loved unconditionally. I think it is safe to say that we crave love and acceptance as a person dying of thirst would crave water. Sadly, people often look for the love they desire in all the wrong places and may even compromise their standards and moral values in order to get it. The only person from whom we can get complete, unconditional love is God. He offers it freely and abundantly at no cost to us except that we believe His promise to give it and then receive it by faith and learn to abide in it continually throughout our lives. This, of course, sounds like good news and as if it should be easy to do, but most people find the opposite to be true. Why?

Our experience with human beings is usually limited: even if they do love us, their love is conditional, based on whether or not we please them. They give us love when we please them and withdraw it when we do not. We quickly learn that love has a price that must be paid on an ongoing basis, so we try hard to be what we think people want us to be in order to obtain the love and acceptance we desire. When people are disappointed in their quest for unconditional love, that deficit in their lives can morph into addictive behaviors aimed at relieving the pain of rejection they feel.

Through Jesus Christ, God has offered a solution to this problem. He offers us what we have been looking for. His love is everlasting, and it is so big that we could never measure how high, deep, long, or wide it is. It makes no sense to us because we know we do not deserve such a love as this, and because it doesn't seem reasonable or possible, we often miss it altogether. But, I urge you to meditate on Ephesians 1:4–6 and other verses I will expound on in Ephesians until the truth of the Scripture becomes a revelation in your heart. I can say with all certainty that nothing else in our lives will ever work properly until we receive God's love by faith. The knowledge that we are loved unconditionally needs to be the solid foundation of our lives. We simply believe it because God said it, and we cease trying to find a reason for it. God loves us because He wants to. It pleases Him to do so.

Personal Reflection

Do you believe that God loves you unconditionally, that He loves you even when you have not behaved well, and that it is impossible for Him to ever stop loving you, because love is not something He merely does; love is who God is (1 John 4:8)?

_____

_____

_____

_____

_____

_____

_____

_____

CHAPTER 2

KNOWING WHO WE ARE IN CHRIST

Our Identity in Him

Ephesians 1:7–10

*In Him we have redemption [that is, our deliverance and
salvation] through His blood, [which paid the penalty
for our sin and resulted in] the forgiveness and complete
pardon of our sin, in accordance with the riches of His grace
which He lavished on us. In all wisdom and understanding
[with practical insight] He made known to us the mystery of
His will according to His good pleasure, which He purposed
in Christ, with regard to the fulfillment of the times [that
is, the end of history, the climax of the ages]—to bring all
things together in Christ, [both] things in the heavens and
things on the earth.*

In these verses we see the phrase "in Him" or "in Christ" several times. Though it is a short phrase, it is one of the most
important ones in the New Testament. It refers to believers being "in Christ." Verse 7 begins with "In Him we have
redemption." Later in the chapter, verse 11 reads "in Him also
we have received an inheritance," and verse 13 tells us that
"in Him" we were stamped with the seal of the Holy Spirit. As
we study God's Word, we see this phrase used many times,
usually attached to a specific promise or piece of good news.

What does it mean to be "in Him"? It means precisely this:

those who, by faith, have received Jesus as their Savior are seen by God as being "in Christ," and because of that, all the wonderful promises referred to are theirs.

In a sense, as God's children we live in two places. The people Paul was writing to lived in Ephesus, but he also wanted them to know that they lived in Christ. I live in St. Louis, Missouri, but I also live in Christ. Our natural life is lived with our feet on the ground, but simultaneously we have another life, a spiritual life, and it is lived in Christ.

A turning point for the children of God comes when we learn who we are "in Christ." I was a Christian for many years before I learned this truth, and as a result I lived in frustration and did not experience any practical victory in my daily life. Many Christians spend their lives trying to get something that is already theirs in Christ. They may try to be right with God through their own good works and behavior, yet they always end up disappointed because they always fail. However, when they see the glorious truth of the gospel and realize that because they are in Christ, God already views them as being in right standing with Him, then their struggle ceases and joy increases. They can learn to rest in the finished work of the cross. While hanging on the cross, Jesus said, "It is finished," and He meant that He has become the propitiation (the payment) for all our sins. It was finished. The door was now open for anyone who would believe to enter into the Holy of Holies and have intimate relationship with God.

Here are ten Scripture-based confessions you can think

about, choose to believe, and speak aloud to affirm who you are in Christ.

1. I am alive with Christ (Eph. 2:5).
2. I am free from the law of sin and death (Rom. 8:2).
3. I am holy and without blame before Him in love (Eph. 1:4; 1 Pet. 1:16).
4. I have the mind of Christ (1 Cor. 2:16; Phil. 2:5).
5. I have the peace of God that surpasses all understanding (Phil. 4:7).
6. I have the Greater One living in me; greater is He who is in me than he who is in the world (1 John 4:4).
7. I can do all things through Christ Jesus (Phil. 4:13).
8. I am a new creature in Christ (2 Cor. 5:17).
9. I am more than a conqueror through Him who loves me (Rom. 8:37).
10. I am the righteousness of God in Christ Jesus (2 Cor. 5:21).

Inheritors and Joint Heirs
Ephesians 1:11–12

In Him also we have received an inheritance [a destiny—we were claimed by God as His own], having been predestined (chosen, appointed beforehand) according to the purpose of Him who works everything in agreement with the counsel and design of His will, so that we who were the first to hope in Christ [who first put our confidence in Him as our Lord and Savior] would exist to the praise of His glory.

In Christ we have obtained an inheritance. When parents leave an inheritance to their children, the sons and daughters receive at no cost what the parents have worked for and earned. That is good news and surely says a lot to the children about how the parents felt about them. It is a cause for rejoicing.

Paul's letter to the Romans states that if we are God's children then we are heirs of God and fellow heirs (joint heirs) with Christ. We share His spiritual blessings and inheritance because of our faith in Him (Rom. 8:17). Jesus said that everything the Father has is His, and that all that is His is ours (John 16:15).

Paul also makes reference to the laborer when writing to the Romans. He says that to the laborer, his wages are not counted as a gift, but as something owed to him (Rom. 4:4). Unless we see what a gift it is for God to view us as being "in Christ," we can never be truly thankful for all God does for us. If we see ourselves as laborers, we will definitely labor, and when we manage to do something we view as good, we will feel that God is obligated by our good works to do something for us. That legalistic attitude regarding our relationship with God causes a great deal of misery for the child of God.

A sixteenth-century monk named Martin Luther experienced the misery of being a spiritual laborer. After feeling this great spiritual agony for many long years, he finally read in Romans 1:17 that "the just shall live by faith" and soon realized that salvation is only by the grace of God through faith, and that it is not, nor can it ever be, obtained by our good works. This revelation eventually brought about the Protestant Reformation, which forever changed how we view our relationship with God.

Once we understand that we cannot earn salvation or right standing with God through any amount of good works, and we fully accept that we are saved and made right with God through Christ and Him alone, only then can we begin to live the way we should as children and representatives of Christ.

Paul devotes a great deal of time in the first three chapters of Ephesians to teach us who we are in Christ. To summarize what he says: we are loved unconditionally, accepted, chosen, and adopted by God, all by His grace and goodness.

The final three chapters of Ephesians are dedicated to teaching us how we should behave in light of who we are in Christ. In fact, we cannot behave according to God's will until and unless we first know this most wonderful and amazing truth. One of the greatest tragedies for children of God is to be taught only how believers should behave without ever learning who we are "in Him."

Personal Reflection

Do you know who you are in Christ?

_____

_____

_____

_____

_____

_____

_____

_____

_____

Sealed with the Holy Spirit
Ephesians 1:13–14

In Him, you also, when you heard the word of truth, the good news of your salvation, and [as a result] believed in Him, were stamped with the seal of the promised Holy Spirit [the One promised by Christ] as owned and protected [by God]. The Spirit is the guarantee [the first installment, the pledge, a foretaste] of our inheritance until the redemption of God's own [purchased] possession [His believers], to the praise of His glory.

Some products we purchase bear a little seal guaranteeing us that the products are good and that we can trust them. The seal means the manufacturer stands behind the products, approves of them, and has arranged for them to be preserved in good condition.

We are told twice in Ephesians and once in Corinthians that the Holy Spirit seals children of God in a similar way. Understanding the culture of Ephesus helps us understand how marvelous this sealing truly is.

Both Ephesus and Corinth were centers of the lumber industry in Paul's day. When logs were brought in on the Black Sea and held on rafts in the harbor, lumber firms sent their representatives to choose and mark (seal as their own) the logs they chose to purchase. As part of the sealing process, the owner paid earnest money to guarantee that he would come for the logs at the right time. Although the logs might sit in the harbor for long periods of time, everyone knew to whom they belonged and for whom they had been separated.

On the final day of our redemption, when Christ returns for us, He will take out of this world all who have been sealed with the Holy Spirit. The sealing of the Holy Spirit guarantees our full inheritance and also preserves us while we are in this world waiting for Christ's return. We need not live in fear, nor should we worry, because we have a guarantee.

The Holy Spirit is the guarantee of our inheritance. His presence in our lives is the down payment of the good things that are to come. God promises that we will acquire full possession of complete redemption from evil and all its consequences. This knowledge should give us great confidence throughout our lives on earth, as well as a happy anticipation of the good things to come that are ours in Christ.

Personal Reflection

How often do you think about the Lord's return and what it is going to be like to see Him as He truly is and to live for all eternity in His manifest presence?

_____

_____

_____

_____

_____

_____

_____

_____

Paul's Prayer for Believers

Ephesians 1:15–20

For this reason, because I have heard of your faith in the Lord Jesus and your love for all God's people, I do not cease to give thanks for you, remembering you in my prayers; [I always pray] that the God of our Lord Jesus Christ, the Father of glory, may grant you a spirit of wisdom and of revelation [that gives you a deep and personal and intimate insight] into the true knowledge of Him [for we know the Father through the Son]. And [I pray] that the eyes of your heart [the very center and core of your being] may be enlightened [flooded with light by the Holy Spirit], so that you will know and cherish the hope [the divine guarantee, the confident expectation] to which He has called you, the riches of His glorious inheritance in the saints (God's people), and [so that you will begin to know] what the immeasurable and unlimited and surpassing greatness of His [active, spiritual] power is in us who believe. These are in accordance with the working of His mighty strength which He produced in Christ when He raised Him from the dead and seated Him at His own right hand in the heavenly places...

Paul had heard about the love and faith of the Ephesian church. I hope that when people hear about us, they will also hear of our love for all people and our faith in the Lord Jesus Christ. Those are the best things to be known for. Have you ever thought about what you would like people to say about you after you are no longer living on Earth? Do you prefer that they say you were wealthy, the president of a major corporation, or perhaps a famous actress or singer? Or would you like them to say about you what Paul was hearing about the Ephesians? Let's remember to focus our lives on what is truly important, on the things that are eternal rather than the ones that are merely temporal.

Paul prayed for the Ephesians all the time, and he said that he gave thanks for them because of their faith and love. He also prayed some other very important things for them, prayers that are quite wonderful if we search their spiritual depth.

Paul did not pray for the Ephesians to be delivered from any and all difficulties or for them to have more material goods. In fact, I can't recall one prayer for anything of this nature in any of Paul's prayers in this Epistle or in the others. I am not saying that it is wrong for us to ask God to help us in our difficulties or to meet our material needs, but those things should not be the ones we focus on most.

Everything Paul prayed for was something that would help the believers spiritually. Paul knew how valuable spiritual strength is and understood that when we are strong spiritually and when we know who we are in Christ, it carries us through circumstantial difficulties all the way to victory.

Being strong in spirit sustains us through bodily pain and in various types of trouble (Prov. 18:14 AMPC). Although our first impulse is to pray for no pain or trouble, it would be far better to pray for spiritual strength to endure whatever comes with good temper. We have no promise from God that we will never have difficulty in this life, but we do have His promises that He will always be with us and He will help and strengthen us (Josh. 1:9; Isa. 41:10; Matt. 28:20).

Paul prayed for us to have a deep and personal understanding regarding the true knowledge of Christ because it is through Him that we know God. Knowing God may sound unattainable, but it is exactly what Paul prayed for. Eternal life is to know God and His Son Jesus Christ (John 17:3). To know Him means to know His character, how He responds to various situations, how He treats people, and what love is—because He is love. To know God is to know life and light and all that is good. Paul stated in his letter to the Philippians that his determined purpose was to know Jesus and the power of His resurrection (Phil. 3:10).

Let us seek God's face and not just His hand, which means to be certain that we seek to know God for who He is rather than merely seeking to know what He can do for us.

Next Paul prayed for us to be enlightened by the Holy Spirit and know the hope (confident expectation) of our calling and how rich the glorious inheritance is that is ours as God's people. If we can sense the passion and depth with which Paul prayed, perhaps we can begin to understand how very important it is for us to know these things in our heart rather than just in our minds. We need to meditate on and study these truths until they become revelation to us instead of just information we have heard about.

Let us get a sense of how glorious, amazing, and beyond full comprehension this inheritance is that we are expecting to receive!

Finally, in this prayer Paul asks that we might know the immeasurable and unlimited power that is available to us who believe. No matter how great our need may be, there is power available to us to match that need. No matter how weak we may feel or how great the temptation that comes against us, there is power available to enable us to meet it with confidence and conquer it.

If the power is available, then why do we so often falter and fail? We fail because we have not been educated regarding this power, we do not truly believe it is available to us, or we do not ask for it and take the time to wait to receive it from God. Power is available to you right now. You do not need to live in weakness and defeat.

Just as Paul's prayers revealed much about his spiritual maturity, priorities, and relationship with God, our prayers reveal much about what is important to us and about our level of spiritual maturity. Let us not read Paul's prayers without taking time to ponder our own. Are our prayers materialistically heavy? Do our prayers reveal that we care more for our material comfort than we do for our spiritual knowledge and strength? If so, we can change that immediately by simply changing how we pray.

Prayer need not be seen as something complicated and perhaps beyond our ability to do properly. For the believer, prayer should be just as natural and simple as breathing. I urge you to pray about everything, anywhere, and all the time. I like to say, "Pray your way through the day." Prayer is having a conversation with God. It should be natural and comfortable. You can talk to God about anything because He already knows everything. Nothing is hidden from Him. Prayer is not only talking; it also involves listening. As you listen, God will speak to your heart and reveal the direction you should take.

If God already knows everything, why should we talk to Him about what He already knows? It is good for us to verbalize and express ourselves. Sharing helps to build relationship. I find it almost impossible to build a friendship with people who never want to share anything personal or meaningful about themselves.

Personal Reflection

Is prayer a lifestyle for you, or is it a spiritual duty or obligation on your daily to-do list?

_____

_____

_____

_____

_____

_____

_____

Christ the Head
Ephesians 1:21–23

*Far above all rule and authority and power and dominion
[whether angelic or human], and [far above] every name
that is named [above every title that can be conferred],
not only in this age and world but also in the one to come.
And He put all things [in every realm] in subjection
under Christ's feet, and appointed Him as [supreme and
authoritative] head over all things in the church, which is
His body, the fullness of Him who fills and completes all
things in all [believers].*

Jesus is the head of all things. He is far above any other
authority or rule, and according to Ephesians 1:22, all things
are under His feet. This is good news for us because not only
is He the head but those who believe in Him are His body. If
you think of this in a practical sense, you can readily understand that what belongs to the head also belongs to the body.
The body takes all its instructions from the head. If I move my
hand, it is because my head has told my arm and my hand to
move. If I walk, it is because my head has instructed my feet
to move forward and take steps. As the psalmist says, we are
fearfully and wonderfully made (Ps. 139:14).

When we as God's children submit to Christ as the head of all our actions, we also share in His authority and power.

We, as Christ's body, are on the earth, and we are the completeness and the full measure of Him. Each of us has a part in God's grand plan. We have gifts and abilities, and as we employ them for the good and benefit of all, Christ is completed in the earth.

We are Christ's personal representatives, and He is making His appeal to the world through us (2 Cor. 5:20). This is a stunningly amazing thought, and it is both a privilege and a great responsibility that we should take seriously.

CHAPTER 3

---◇---

PAST, PRESENT,
AND FUTURE

Who We Were, Who We Are, and Who We Will Be

Ephesians 2:1–7

*And you [He made alive when you] were [spiritually] dead
and separated from Him because of your transgressions and
sins, in which you once walked. You were following the ways
of this world [influenced by this present age], in accordance
with the prince of the power of the air (Satan), the spirit who
is now at work in the disobedient [the unbelieving, who fight
against the purposes of God]. Among these [unbelievers]
we all once lived in the passions of our flesh [our behavior
governed by the sinful self], indulging the desires of human
nature [without the Holy Spirit] and [the impulses] of the
[sinful] mind. We were, by nature, children [under the
sentence] of [God's] wrath, just like the rest [of mankind].
But God, being [so very] rich in mercy, because of His great
and wonderful love with which He loved us, even when we
were [spiritually] dead and separated from Him because of
our sins, He made us [spiritually] alive together with Christ
(for by His grace—His undeserved favor and mercy—you
have been saved from God's judgment). And He raised us
up together with Him [when we believed], and seated us
with Him in the heavenly places, [because we are] in Christ
Jesus, [and He did this] so that in the ages to come He might
[clearly] show the immeasurable and unsurpassed riches*

of His grace in [His] kindness toward us in Christ Jesus [by providing for our redemption].

In today's world, multitudes of people seek fortune-tellers, psychics, and mediums, trying to get a glimpse into their future or to understand situations and issues from their past or in their present situation. God's Word teaches us that it is offensive to God for people to do that because He wants them to seek Him (Lev. 19:26, 31). He has all the answers to our past, present, and future, and Ephesians 2 reveals this.

Before we came alive in Christ, we were spiritually dead and separated from God because of sin. We walked in sin and followed the ways of the world. By doing so, we were unknowingly following the ways of Satan, the evil spirit who works in and through all unbelievers and who fights against God's purpose and will. We walked in sin, perhaps not even aware we were sinning because we were dead to God, spiritually speaking. We had no relationship with God and were not in any way guided and led by His Spirit. If you remember your life before you accepted Jesus as your Savior, I am sure you remember that it was a miserable existence that was without peace and joy.

But God intervened, and even when we did not care about Him at all, He cared about us. Through Christ He arranged for us to be delivered from the misery of sin and separation from Him. Jesus paid for you and me to be spiritually alive in Him, to be completely forgiven of our sin and given a new life in Christ. Jesus did everything because He loves us, and now all we need to do is believe and surrender our lives to Him. The Ephesians had already believed and surrendered their lives to God through Christ, and Paul reminds them of what an amazing gift this is.

Paul uses only two short words to open Ephesians 2:4, but they are powerful words indeed. "But God" means that God interrupted the mess mankind was in and because of His love He provided an answer to the dilemma. The phrase "but God" is the transition from hopelessness to hope and from complete negativity to positivity. The people were dead in sin, but God intervened and raised them up and seated them in heavenly places because they were in Christ, and all of this is true today for everyone who believes.

We see the phrase "but God" used a few times in Scripture, and in each instance we see God's delivering power (1 Sam. 23:14; Ps. 49:15; Ps. 73:26; Rom. 5:8).

For example, Joseph's brothers hated him and tried to do everything they could to destroy him, *but God* was with him (Acts 7:9). If you know the story of Joseph you know that although overwhelming odds were seemingly against him, he still succeeded and became great because even though many were against him, God was for him.

God is for you, too, and because He is, you can overcome any obstacle in your path.

Joseph's brothers meant evil in their treatment of him, *but God* meant it for good so that many people should be kept alive during a great famine that came upon Egypt (Gen.

50:20). His brothers sold him into slavery, and he ended up in Egypt, the place where God had destined him to become great.

As another example, the apostle John writes that the devil comes to kill, steal, and destroy, *but Jesus* came that we might have and enjoy life (John 10:10).

No matter how much Satan seeks our harm and destruction, God always has a plan for our rescue and victory.

God not only raised us up when we were dead in sin, but He gave us the very life of Christ and He seated us in heavenly places. What does it mean to be seated in heavenly places with Christ? I don't want you to miss the power of this truth.

When Jesus had accomplished all that His Father sent Him to do, the Father raised Jesus up and seated Him at His own right hand, to wait for His enemies to become a footstool for His feet (Heb. 10:12–13). In other words, Jesus is now at perfect rest and peace, and if we are seated with Him, then that same rest and peace is available to us. The next time you start to get upset about something in your life, remind your emotions to take their seat in Christ and trust Him to do what you cannot do. You once had to worry and be anxious, but now that you are in Christ, you can rest in Him.

Personal Reflection

Are there times in your life when you could and should take your seat in Christ and wait for Him to make your enemies a footstool for your feet instead of fretting, worrying, being anxious, and taking matters into your own hands? What are they?

_____

_____

_____

_____

_____

_____

_____

What about our future? God also foretells our future, and it is glorious. Paul wrote that in "the ages to come" (the Greek expression for eternity), God will exhibit the full riches of His grace toward us. You and I as children of God are going to be part of a great exhibit in which God shows His magnificence. We have His Spirit as a down payment of the good things that are to come. Our lives are so much better with Christ than they were when we were living in sin, and that is merely a taste of what is to come.

When John was taken into the heavens while on the Isle of Patmos, he saw things he could not even describe because of their magnificence. Looking forward to these things can give us hope in this present time while we wait for Christ's future return.

CHAPTER 4

GOD MADE US AND HE GIVES US HOPE IN CHRIST

God's Workmanship

Ephesians 2:8–10

For it is by grace [God's remarkable compassion and favor drawing you to Christ] that you have been saved [actually delivered from judgment and given eternal life] through faith. And this [salvation] is not of yourselves [not through your own effort], but it is the [undeserved, gracious] gift of God; not as a result of [your] works [nor your attempts to keep the Law], so that no one will [be able to] boast or take credit in any way [for his salvation]. For we are His workmanship [His own master work, a work of art], created in Christ Jesus [reborn from above—spiritually transformed, renewed, ready to be used] for good works, which God prepared [for us] beforehand [taking paths which He set], so that we would walk in them [living the good life which He prearranged and made ready for us].

These are some of the most magnificent and hope-filled verses in God's Word. We don't have to try to work for and earn salvation, because it is a free gift of God's grace that can only be received by faith. Jesus bought our salvation, and faith in Him is the hand that reaches out to receive it.

Although these verses are so simple, many have great difficulty fully believing them and continue to try to earn salvation and right standing with God through their good works. Since that is not God's plan, it will never succeed, and the Bible tells us that anyone who tries to come to God through fulfilling the Law is "cursed (condemned to destruction)" (Gal. 3:10).

There was a time when I tried to earn my way to salvation, as you may have, and I was repeatedly disappointed and extremely frustrated. The only way we can be saved is by grace through faith. There is no other way. It is totally useless to try to buy something that is free and can never be purchased. We cannot buy salvation or right standing with God through good works, giving to the poor, diligence in prayer and Bible study, or following any rules or laws that any person or church may suggest.

We have all sinned and fall short of the glory of God; therefore, all are justified and made right with God through His grace (Rom. 3:23–24). No one can take glory to himself or take credit for what God has done. There is a pride factor in our flesh that wants to earn, deserve, brag, boast, compare, and compete, but God will have none of it. We must humble ourselves and come to Him with nothing to offer except faith in Jesus.

Paul did not say that by grace you are *being* saved, or that you *shall be* saved, but you *have been* saved. Salvation is an established work (something already finished), leaving no room for us to try to work for it because God has already given it. If I give my daughter a lovely gift, it has already been paid for and there is no way she can pay for it again. We cannot pay for our salvation because Jesus has already paid, but we can and should respond in love and with a deep desire to be pleasing to Him in all our ways.

We have been re-created in Christ, born again so we may do the good works God planned for us and desires us to do. As born-again children of God we have new desires and new goals. That may seem like a paradox, but it simply means this: our good works can never in any way earn our salvation or forgiveness of sin, but Christianity without good works is no kind of Christianity at all.

Good works should be the result of Christianity—works that issue from a heart that wants to do them, never from the idea that they must be done to gain something from God. No amount of good works can make God indebted to us, but we can respond to His great and amazing love and gift of salvation by freely choosing to walk the path He planned for us to walk, doing the good works He planned for us to do before the beginning of time.

The Importance of Motive

The motives behind what we do are very important. The work we do is not as important as the reason we do it. Do we make an effort daily to please God because we just want to get something from Him, or because we want to give something to Him? Paul told the Corinthians that any work they did without a pure motive would be burned up on Judgment Day and all reward would be lost (1 Cor. 3:13–15).

I recall reading this as a young Christian and being impacted by the thought that I needed to examine the motives behind all my works. This principle has helped me through-out my life to make sure that my works are Spirit-led and not motivated by selfish desire.

It is sobering to ponder that what we are doing in life may be useless if the motive behind it is impure. Ask yourself if what you are doing is the will of God and is being done for His glory, or if it is being done to impress other people or, even worse, as an attempt to impress God, hoping to gain something from Him.

Here are a few questions to consider:

- Do you spend time with God because you think you have to, or because you truly want to be with Him?
- Do you read and study the Bible in order to fulfill an obligation you feel you have to God, or because you truly love His Word and want to learn what His will is in all things?
- Do you pray because you realize you can do nothing without God and because doing so is a privilege, or do you pray to fulfill a duty?
- Do you serve and do good works because you truly want to help people as a service to God, or because you think good works will make God indebted to you?

These may be difficult questions to answer, but doing so can be one of the most important and freeing things that you ever do. Being brutally honest with yourself is one of the most valuable things that you can do, because only truth will make you free (John 8:32).

Personal Reflection

Think about or discuss with someone the major things you spend your time doing, and then ask yourself why you are doing them. If you are willing to eliminate everything that is done with impure motives, you may suddenly find that your schedule is no longer overcrowded and stressful.

_____

_____

_____

_____

_____

_____

_____

_____

We Have Hope

Ephesians 2:11–12

Therefore, remember that at one time you Gentiles by birth, who are called "Uncircumcision" by those who called themselves "Circumcision," [itself a mere mark] which is made in the flesh by human hands—remember that at that time you were separated from Christ [excluded from any relationship with Him], alienated from the commonwealth of Israel, and strangers to the covenants of promise [with no share in the sacred Messianic promise and without knowledge of God's agreements], having no hope [in His promise] and [living] in the world without God.

Paul reminds the Ephesian Christians of the terrible condition they were in spiritually before they were saved by God's grace. Although he has already covered this thoroughly, he now covers it again. He reminds them of the following facts:

- They were separated from God.
- They walked in the flesh.
- They were rejected and criticized.
- They had no knowledge of God's promises, and no share in them.
- They had no hope and were in the world without God.

What was true for the Ephesians is true for us, too. Just think about the terrible and hopeless condition we were in, and many are still in today. But thank God we were born again into a living hope and we now have joy and peace because of the grace of God.

We Have Been Brought Near

Ephesians 2:13–16

*But now [at this very moment] in Christ Jesus you who
once were [so very] far away [from God] have been brought
near by the blood of Christ. For He Himself is our peace
and our bond of unity. He who made both groups—[Jews
and Gentiles]—into one body and broke down the barrier,
the dividing wall [of spiritual antagonism between us],
by abolishing in His [own crucified] flesh the hostility
caused by the Law with its commandments contained in
ordinances [which He satisfied]; so that in Himself He might
make the two into one new man, thereby establishing peace.
And [that He] might reconcile them both [Jew and Gentile,
united] in one body to God through the cross, thereby
putting to death the hostility.*

But now we have been brought near. Even though we were
previously far away from God because of our sin, now by
the blood of Jesus we have been brought near. We can have
a close and intimate relationship with God. We have been
offered peace with God.

The Ephesian Christians were Gentiles. According to
the circumcised Jews, they were the uncircumcised. This
means the Israelites (Jews) were in covenant with God, and

circumcision was something that God required as an outward
sign of their agreement to follow His laws (rules and regula-
tions). They saw anyone who was outside of this covenant as
being Gentiles and referred to them as "the uncircumcised."
Their attitude toward uncircumcised people was not good.
They felt they were better than the rest of mankind. Not only
were they entrenched in their pride, but their pride also separated them from other people and caused them to reject the
idea that others could be included in the covenant with God
by and through their example and lovingkindness.

Once Christ fulfilled the law and introduced the covenant
of grace, there was no need for circumcision, but some of
the Jews continued to tell the Gentile converts that they still
needed it in order to be proper Christians.

Paul preached that we are saved totally by grace and not by
works, yet some of the Jews had taken so much pride in their
works for so long that they could not comprehend this new
doctrine. They had erected a dividing wall between themselves and people from other nations and cultures for centuries. But, as we shall see, Christ tore down this dividing wall
by fulfilling the law for us.

Our world today is filled with division, strife, and enmity.
It exists between races of people, between nations, between
religions and Christian denominations, and between the rich
and the poor, the educated and uneducated, male and female.
Just think for a moment about how much turmoil the world is
in constantly due to pride that causes division.

Personal Reflection

I urge you to search your heart and ask God to show you if you have erected any dividing walls between yourself and other people due to pride.

_____

_____

_____

_____

_____

_____

_____

Satan loves division because he knows that it weakens us and causes us to be ineffective. God loves unity and teaches us that where unity exists, there is anointing (the power and presence of God) and blessing (Ps. 133). Jesus even told His disciples when He sent them out two by two to minister to people and prepare them before He came to them that they had to remain in peace (Luke 10:1–12). If we have no peace, then we have no power.

Jesus left us His own special peace when He ascended on high and also expressed the importance of holding on to it (John 14:27). Where strife exists, pride is always the root cause of the problem (Prov. 13:10). Pride—especially spiritual pride—was a huge problem for the Jews, and it remains a problem today, but it need not be a problem if we all remember that Christ is our peace and He has torn down the dividing walls by letting us know that our worth and value is not in what we do or can ever do, but it is "in Him."

The Jews needed to realize that they could not keep the law perfectly no matter how hard they tried and that they needed Jesus just as much as everyone else did. The Gentiles needed to realize that even though they had not been part of the Old Covenant of law and works, they were now being offered a New Covenant of salvation by grace through faith in Jesus Christ.

Jesus' Message Is for Everyone

Ephesians 2:17–22

AND HE CAME AND PREACHED THE GOOD NEWS OF PEACE TO YOU *[Gentiles]* WHO WERE FAR AWAY, AND PEACE TO THOSE *[Jews]* WHO WERE NEAR. *For it is through Him that we both have a [direct] way of approach in one Spirit to the Father. So then you are no longer strangers and aliens [outsiders without rights of citizenship], but you are fellow citizens with the saints (God's people), and are [members] of God's household, having been built on the foundation of the apostles and prophets, with Christ Jesus Himself as the [chief] Cornerstone, in whom the whole structure is joined together, and it continues [to increase] growing into a holy temple in the Lord [a sanctuary dedicated, set apart, and sacred to the presence of the Lord]. In Him [and in fellowship with one another] you also are being built together into a dwelling place of God in the Spirit.*

Jesus preached the same message of peace to Jew and Gentile alike. He had come to kill the hostility that divided them. Through Him they both had access to the Father. Those who had been outsiders were now included in the household of God.

Have you ever felt like an outsider, as if you didn't belong or weren't welcome? Most of us have felt that way at some time, and it is exactly how Satan wants us to feel. He hopes we will feel either inferior or superior, and he doesn't care which one it is as long as it brings division. But in Christ no one is inferior or superior; instead we are all one in Him. Paul taught that there is no more Jew or Gentile, slave or free, male or female, but we are all one in Christ (Gal. 3:28).

Our confidence and security is in Christ and in Him alone. It cannot be found in our performance or any other so-called advantage we may have. Paul said that he was more than happy to count all of his advantages as a Jew as rubbish (garbage) compared to the priceless privilege of knowing Christ Jesus and being found and known as "in Him" (Phil. 3:8–10).

CHAPTER 5

THE COST, THE MYSTERY, AND THE POWER OF THE GOSPEL

Suffering for the Sake of the Gospel
Ephesians 3:1

For this reason [because I preach that you and believing
Jews are joint heirs] I, Paul, am the prisoner of Christ Jesus
on behalf of you Gentiles.

Paul was in prison when he wrote this letter to the Ephesians
and the other churches that ultimately received it. But, notice
that he calls himself a "prisoner of Christ Jesus." He wasn't
saying that the Lord had put him in prison, but that he was
there for preaching the gospel of Christ and was more than
willing to stay there if it resulted in people coming to believe
in Jesus.

Perhaps we should ask ourselves occasionally how much
we are willing to suffer in order to help spread the good
news of the gospel. When God called me to teach His Word,
friends, church, and family rejected me because of it. I suffered rejection and a great deal of misunderstanding, yet all I
wanted to do was follow God and help people.

Sadly, doing the right thing does not always produce an
immediate positive response from the people we know. Many
have experienced the type of rejection I did, or they have
lost jobs or been persecuted in other ways because of their
bold commitment to Jesus. Although the pain of rejection is

difficult to go through, it does allow us to fellowship with Christ in His sufferings (Phil. 3:10) and complete what remains to be done for the sake of spreading the message of salvation. We are co-laborers with Christ, and that means we have the privilege of continuing the work He began and then turned over to the apostles to continue.

In our Western culture we are not good at being uncomfortable. We are addicted to convenience and quite often don't behave well when we need to do without it. Peter said that Christ suffered in the flesh for us and that we should arm ourselves with the same thought and purpose: "being willing to suffer for doing what is right and pleasing God" (1 Pet. 4:1).

Many people are suffering today around the world, and some are being killed because of their faith in Christ. You or I may never be required to do that, but at the very least we should be willing to be judged critically or rejected or misunderstood, should that be required of us.

We are to be God pleasers, not people pleasers. Paul said that had he been trying to be popular with people, he would not have been an apostle of the Lord (Gal. 1:10). I urge you to take a strong stand concerning your faith in Jesus Christ and be willing to lose anything other than that. Don't compromise with the world and its ways, but stand strong and keep growing in God. Don't be lukewarm, but be fully committed to following Jesus with all your heart.

Personal Reflection

Are you a people pleaser or a God pleaser? If you want to be more of a God pleaser, how can you accomplish that?

_____

_____

_____

_____

_____

_____

_____

_____

The Mystery

Ephesians 3:2–6

Assuming that you have heard of the stewardship of God's grace that was entrusted to me [to share with you] for your benefit; and that by [divine] revelation the mystery was made known to me, as I have already written in brief. By referring to this, when you read it you can understand my insight into the mystery of Christ, which in other generations was not disclosed to mankind, as it has now been revealed to His holy apostles and prophets by the [Holy] Spirit; [it is this:] that the Gentiles are now joint heirs [with the Jews] and members of the same body, and joint partakers [sharing] in the [same divine] promise in Christ Jesus through [their faith in] the good news [of salvation].

The Gentiles becoming fellow heirs with the Jews was a mystery. It was a cultural shock to Jew and Gentile alike—more than we can even imagine. The Jews had worked hard and tried to follow the laws of God for centuries, and now the Gentiles, who had never done that, were to be given the same benefits as the Jews.

An example that might help us understand this is pondering how the oldest child in a family, after he has worked hard, sacrificed, and perhaps done without many things because his parents could not afford to provide them, feels toward the baby of the family, who was born at a time when Mom and Dad had more money and life was much easier. This often creates sibling rivalry and resentment.

The Jews had worked hard for what the Gentiles were being given, but they had not come to realize that even though they had worked hard to keep the law, all have sinned and come short of the glory of God, and all need to be justified and made right with God by faith in Christ (Rom. 3:23–24).

God only gave the law to show the Jews that they could not keep it—they could never make themselves right with God in their own strength or effort—and they needed a Savior. They needed the Messiah who had been promised to them (Gal. 3:19). Their mistake was in not realizing that they were just as guilty as the Gentiles, because if one attempted to be right with God through the law, he had to keep every point of the law and not make even one tiny mistake. Of course, that was impossible (James 2:10). In reality, we are all equal because we all need Jesus, and without Him we have no hope of having a right relationship with God.

We Can Do Nothing without Christ

Ephesians 3:7–11

Of this [gospel] I was made a minister by the gift of God's grace given me through the working of His power. To me, [though I am] the very least of all the saints (God's people), this grace [which is undeserved] was graciously given, to proclaim to the Gentiles the good news of the incomprehensible riches of Christ [that spiritual wealth which no one can fully understand], and to make plain [to everyone] the plan of the mystery [regarding the uniting of believing Jews and Gentiles into one body] which [until now] was kept hidden through the ages in [the mind of] God who created all things. So now through the church the multifaceted wisdom of God [in all its countless aspects] might now be made known [revealing the mystery] to the [angelic] rulers and authorities in the heavenly places. This is in accordance with [the terms of] the eternal purpose which He carried out in Christ Jesus our Lord.

Paul expresses that grace alone made him a minister, and that God's power gave him the gifts he needed to do what God was asking him to do. He says with humility that he is the least of all the saints, making it clear that he does not think himself to be better than anyone else because of the revelations God has given him.

It is very important that we never see ourselves as better than others. When we do, we are guilty of pride. That kind of pride will cause us to have an attitude toward people that is not pleasing to God. Paul reminds us often in his letters to be humble and not to think more highly of ourselves than we ought, but to realize that our abilities are given to us by God (Rom. 12:3).

Personal Reflection

Do you fully realize that all of your gifts, talents, and abilities are gifts from God and should in no way make you feel superior to anyone else?

_____

_____

_____

_____

_____

_____

_____

_____

_____

We all have gifts from God, but they are not all the same. Each one is valuable, and we are to share them with one another, thereby enabling all believers to work together in order to see God's will done on earth. His great dream is to see all people unified in Him and fulfilling the purpose for which He has created them.

God wants all of us to understand the mystery regarding the unification of the Jews and Gentiles, as well as all other people. Jesus stated that we are all one in Him. There is to be no division between Jew and Greek (Gentile), slave or free, male or female, for we are all equal in Him (Gal. 3:28).

Not only did the Jews see themselves as better than other races of people and nations, but the men believed they were much better than women. Women had few opportunities and were very rarely educated. Divorce was easy for a man, but impossible for a woman, and women had no property rights. Although we do see examples of women in positions of authority, it was very rare. Now Jesus declares afresh what God said at the beginning of time: He created men and women as equals, although they have different roles. Jesus tore down all walls dividing classes and types of people. When walls do exist, it is because we have erected them, and only we can tear them down by walking in love rather than having critical, judgmental attitudes that bring division.

Sometimes the history of Christianity is presented in a

way that makes it sound as if the gospel was preached only to the Gentiles because the Jews would not receive it, but this is inaccurate. Paul reminds us that the Gentiles were not an afterthought in the mind of God. Bringing all people into the great love of God was always His design.

We Can Draw Near to God

Ephesians 3:11–12

This is in accordance with [the terms of] the eternal purpose which He carried out in Christ Jesus our Lord, in whom we have boldness and confident access through faith in Him [that is, our faith gives us sufficient courage to freely and openly approach God through Christ].

All that Paul has written so far has brought us to these great verses, which are some of the most important in the Bible. They are so vital because in the Old Testament, God is seen as unapproachable. The Israelites worshipped in a temple made with hands, which contained three compartments. God's presence dwelt in the innermost sanctuary, called the Holy of Holies. Only the high priest could go into the Holy of Holies, and only once a year to make atonement for his sins and the sins of the people. However, Paul speaks of God as our Father and brings us the good news that because of our faith in Jesus, we may now approach God with courage and confidence. We have free, unreserved access to God.

The very center of the Christian faith is the approachability of God. We can approach Him at any time and talk to Him about anything, and we will never be rejected. I am sure this idea was shocking to the Jews, because they had never enjoyed this kind of intimacy with God. If we do not understand the importance of verse 12, we may fail to receive all that God has for us simply because we are unaware that we can ask, and ask boldly, for anything we need. God is interested in everything about us.

We have the great privilege of intimate fellowship with God. He wants to be involved in all aspects of our lives, not merely the spiritual ones. And we should always approach Him with reverence and respect, keeping in mind that He is also our Father and friend.

Personal Reflection

When you approach God in prayer, do you come boldly and confidently, or sheepishly, wondering whether or not God will hear you?

_____

_____

_____

_____

_____

_____

_____

CHAPTER 6

—◇—

BOLDNESS, STABILITY, AND LOVE

Praying Boldly

Ephesians 3:13

So I ask you not to lose heart at my sufferings on your behalf, for they are your glory and honor.

Although Paul was suffering in prison for preaching the gospel, he did not want the people to become fearful and discouraged because of what he was going through. Paul didn't mind the suffering since he was enduring it to help them. He wanted them to be strengthened by his ordeal rather than weakened by it. Sometimes if we see someone go through difficulty and emerge victorious, it encourages us that we can do the same, and that is what Paul wanted for the Christians.

Paul deeply loved the people he had been called to minister to, and he was willing to do whatever he needed to do, even if it meant personal sacrifice, in order to help them and fulfill God's purpose for his life.

We will all encounter times when we must be willing to endure difficulty for the sake of the gospel. It may not be imprisonment like Paul experienced—although people do experience this in some parts of the world today—but no matter what it is, we should glory in it and believe that God has a purpose for it and that He will use it for our good and the good of His Kingdom.

People often experience rejection or some other type of persecution from others because of their Christianity. Although that is very painful, we can compare that to what Paul suffered and be encouraged to press on boldly.

Paul continues in his letter with another of his great prayers for the people. He apparently sees great value in praying for them, because he does it frequently. However, it is not the frequency of his prayers that interests me most; it is how he prays and what he asks God to do for them. The prayers of Paul can be models for us to follow when praying for others as well as for ourselves. There are times when we want to pray for someone and yet we don't know how to pray or what to ask for, but the types of prayers we see in this text are powerful beyond our imagination.

Strength and Stability

Ephesians 3:14–16

For this reason [grasping the greatness of this plan by which Jews and Gentiles are joined together in Christ] I bow my knees [in reverence] before the Father [of our Lord Jesus Christ], from whom every family in heaven and on earth derives its name [God—the first and ultimate Father]. May He grant you out of the riches of His glory, to be strengthened and spiritually energized with power through His Spirit in your inner self, [indwelling your innermost being and personality].

Paul begins by praying for something most of us pray for often, and that is strength. We need strength in many areas of our lives, yet the type of strength Paul prays for is definitely the most important: strength for the inner self. When we speak of the inner self, we are referring to our inmost being, which encompasses our thoughts, emotions, will, and conscience. Inner strength carries us through life's difficulties and challenges while allowing us to remain joyful.

We often pray for physical strength to be able to carry on with a project that has left us tired and fatigued, and it is right to do so, but strength in the inner self is even more valuable. When we are strong inwardly, that strength often manifests in determination that carries us through to victory in spite of many hardships.

It is important for Christians to be an example to others of how to live. One of the things people need to see in us is stability. If our temperament and commitment are ever-changing based on our circumstances, then God cannot use us to draw others to Himself. Stability is something the world desperately needs, and we need to model it for them. This stability comes from inner fortitude, not physical strength. As an example, think about this: no matter how many times a week I go to the gym and lift weights to build muscle, it will not help me be emotionally stable during hard times.

Whenever you or someone you know is experiencing a great trial—whether physically, mentally, emotionally, financially, within a relationship, or in any other way—the best way to pray is just as Paul did in this amazing prayer. Pray for inner strength and for mighty power. Pray for the power of God to fill your (or their) innermost being.

I particularly love this translation from the Amplified Bible, which includes the word *personality*. It is through our personality that we express ourselves. Our thoughts and attitudes toward everything are expressed through our personality, and having a personality that is Spirit-filled sounds amazingly good to me.

Just imagine how much better relationships would be if we all had Spirit-filled personalities. That, of course, means that God and His ways could be seen in and through us daily as we interact with others. Surely, we can see the importance of this prayer Paul prayed. He was certainly led by the Holy Spirit in his praying.

As I ponder how I might have prayed for the people, it may have been for them to be protected from difficulty and to be delivered from their trials, but Paul saw something much better and much more valuable. Why pray for every little difficulty that comes our way to be removed? Would it not be better to pray that we would be so strong in our inner selves that we would barely even notice the hardships and certainly would not be affected by them? We could continue having peace and joy while walking in love toward others.

I pray often for inner strength, perhaps several times each day, because we have an enemy, the devil, who is focused on our destruction. In order to defeat him, we will need a great deal of power on the inside. Therefore I suggest to you that strength is possibly one of the most important things Christians can and should pray for.

Personal Reflection

Do you regularly pray for inner strength?

_____

_____

_____

_____

_____

_____

_____

_____

_____

Rooted Deep in Love

Ephesians 3:16–21

May He grant you... to be strengthened... in your inner self... so that Christ may dwell in your hearts through your faith. And may you, having been [deeply] rooted and [securely] grounded in love, be fully capable of comprehending with all the saints (God's people) the width and length and height and depth of His love [fully experiencing that amazing, endless love]; and [that you may come] to know [practically, through personal experience] the love of Christ which far surpasses [mere] knowledge [without experience], that you may be filled up [throughout your being] to all the fullness of God [so that you may have the richest experience of God's presence in your lives, completely filled and flooded with God Himself]. Now to Him who is able to [carry out His purpose and] do superabundantly more than all that we dare ask or think [infinitely beyond our greatest prayers, hopes, or dreams], according to His power that is at work within us, to Him be the glory in the church and in Christ Jesus throughout all generations forever and ever. Amen.

Christ wants to dwell in our hearts, to be enthroned in our hearts by faith. We may not always feel that Christ dwells in us, but it is vital for us to know by faith that He does. I like to remind myself of what belongs to me according to God's Word, so I often say to myself, "God is with me right now." I am especially diligent to do so if at any time I start to feel alone or weary.

God is love, and that means that we always have His love in us, just as we also have His presence and power. Jesus told us to abide (live, dwell, and remain) in His love (John 15:9).

We are to know the love of God in a deep and experiential way and to be deeply rooted in it. If we are, it makes us secure just as a tree with deep roots is secure, stable, and strong, even during storms. The deeper its roots, the more difficult it is to uproot and destroy it. One of the best ways I know to become deeply rooted in God's love is to meditate on it frequently and learn to look for signs of it on a daily basis. Let us learn to be conscious and aware of God's love at all times.

In Paul's letter to the Romans he encouraged them to not let anything separate them from the love of God that is found in Christ Jesus: not tribulation, or distress, or persecution, or famine, or anything else (Rom. 8:35–39). When we have problems, they should drive us deeper into God, not away from Him. He is not the source of our problems; He is the answer to them. God's Word does not guarantee us a life with no trials and disappointments, but it does assure us of God's love and guarantees we will never be alone. Your worst day with Jesus will be better than your best day was without Him.

The apostle Paul doesn't want us to merely know about God's love, but to have personal experience with it. He said that experience is much better than mere knowledge. Knowing God's love in this way makes us bold in prayer, and seeing answers to our prayers helps us know even more deeply the great and endless love of God. There is never one moment in our lives when God doesn't love us. He reveals His love to each of us in many ways, but, sadly, we may be unconscious and unaware of it, or even worse we may become so accustomed to the many things that God does for us that we begin to take them for granted.

May we be completely filled and flooded with God and His love, filled to such a degree that His love flows out of us to others and back to God in praise and adoration. We love Him because He first loved us (1 John 4:19).

This love that God has for us and wants us to have for others is not so much an emotion as it is an action, doing things for the benefit of another person and having unselfish concern for them. It is a willingness to seek the very best for another person. This is the quality of love that God has for us and that He desires that we have for one another. If we don't first receive it from God and experience it for ourselves, we will never be able to give it to anyone else. We cannot give what we do not have.

God always provides all we need by His grace, and He never asks us to do for another what He has not first done for us. He gives us mercy and asks us to give it to others, He forgives us and asks us to forgive, and He is kind and asks us to be the same. He loves us unconditionally and asks us to love in the same way. Always remember that the more time you spend receiving and abiding in God's love, the more you will be able to let it flow through you to other people.

Knowing we are loved gives us confidence and boldness and allows us to pray without fear of displeasing God. God wants to do more for us than we can think or imagine. The more God does for us, the more we are able to do for others. I am not speaking only of material things we ask for, but also of things such as peace and joy. The more peace we have from God, the more peace we can bring into each situation we encounter. Jesus could speak peace to the storm when He and His disciples were on the Sea of Galilee because He had peace (Mark 4:35–41).

People who have deep roots pray for deeper things. They don't stay on the surface level of life, asking only for what makes them comfortable and enables them to have all they want. When Peter and the other disciples had been fishing all night and caught nothing, Jesus told them to go out into deeper water and lower their nets again. When they obeyed, they caught so many fish that their nets would not hold them. They had such an overflow that they had to call others to come and fill their boats also (Luke 5:1–7). We can have that same overflow in our lives if we will begin to pray deeper prayers and ask for greater things. We do not have because we do not ask (James 4:2). So I say, let us be confident in God's love and start being bold and daring in our prayers so that God can be glorified through us!

Personal Reflection

Do you consistently know that God loves you no matter what your circumstances look like? Have you experienced His love, and do you see signs of His love in your daily life?

_____

_____

_____

_____

_____

_____

_____

_____

CHAPTER 7

OUR EXAMPLE TO THE WORLD

Proper Christian Behavior

Ephesians 4:1–6

So I, the prisoner for the Lord, appeal to you to live a life worthy of the calling to which you have been called [that is, to live a life that exhibits godly character, moral courage, personal integrity, and mature behavior—a life that expresses gratitude to God for your salvation], with all humility [forsaking self-righteousness], and gentleness [maintaining self-control], with patience, bearing with one another in [unselfish] love. Make every effort to keep the oneness of the Spirit in the bond of peace [each individual working together to make the whole successful]. There is one body [of believers] and one Spirit—just as you were called to one hope when called [to salvation]—one Lord, one faith, one baptism, one God and Father of us all who is [sovereign] over all and [working] through all and [living] in all.

Ephesians has focused to this point on our position and privileges in Christ and on what He has done for us by His grace. Now the apostle Paul begins to write about how we should live in light of the great things God has done for us. We can never do the right things unless God has made us right in our hearts, and He has done that by giving us His beloved Son, Jesus Christ. He is our right standing with God, our peace, and our joy.

The doctrines of our faith are made clear in Ephesians 1–3. Now we turn our attention to how we should live and what our example to the world should be. Strong doctrine alone is not enough; we also need to exercise and demonstrate the practical aspects of our Christian faith. God makes His appeal to people who are not in relationship with Him through people who are. The only way nonbelievers can see God may be through those of us who have Him in our hearts. We are God's representatives on earth, and because of that our behavior is extremely important.

The reputation of the church has been severely damaged by people who know the right things to do but fail to do them. Their doctrine may be right, but their behavior is not. They are often very proud of what they think they know and are quick to tell others what they should do, while not doing it themselves. We need both strong, accurate doctrine and behavior that backs up what we say we believe.

Paul appeals to (begs) the believers to live with behavior that will be a credit to God and represent Him well. As Christians we are followers of Christ, and we should aspire to behave as He did while He was on earth. Becoming more and more like Christ should be our purpose and goal as we live our daily lives.

We need moral courage in order to live among people who don't believe in God. We must be brave and strong, not compromising to win their favor or accommodate their opinions. We should all have a moral standard by which to live, and we should hold firmly to it, even if doing so means personal sacrifice.

We can be sure that Satan will tempt us to compromise, but God delights in those who have personal integrity and consistently do what they believe to be right and proper according to God's Word. It is not how we live occasionally that makes us morally brave. It is not merely doing right when doing so is easy, but doing it consistently, especially when it is difficult. According to Galatians 6:9, if we don't become weary in doing what is right, we will reap good results in due season.

Personal Reflection

In what practical ways can you demonstrate your faith in God and your understanding of what He has done for you in Christ? How should your behavior reflect God's love and goodness to you?

_____

_____

_____

_____

_____

_____

_____

_____

_____

We can learn an important lesson about Christian behavior from the New Testament story of the fig tree. While Jesus was traveling one day, He saw a fig tree with leaves on it. When He approached the tree, expecting to find fruit, there was none. So He cursed the tree, and it withered. When His disciples saw this, they were astonished, and they asked how it had happened. Jesus proceeded to teach them a lesson about faith and prayer. Many scholars comment on the teaching of the fig tree only as a lesson in faith. Although faith is certainly one lesson Jesus taught through this situation, I believe there is another important one that is often missed.

Jesus saw the leaves on the fig tree and knew that when fig trees have leaves, fruit is supposed to be underneath the leaves. But this one had no fruit. Jesus went to the tree expecting to find something to satisfy His hunger, but He left as hungry as He was when He approached it. It had leaves, but no fruit (Matt. 21:19–22).

Many people who call themselves Christians are like that fig tree. They display outward signs indicating that they are Christians—regular church attendance, perhaps a bumper sticker that says something about Jesus, maybe many different Bible translations and a large library filled with books written by Christian authors. They might wear a necklace with a cross on it, displaying the emblem of Christianity, or they may even wear a T-shirt with a Scripture verse printed on it. While these things may be good in themselves, without the fruit of good behavior, they are worthless and may even do harm to the cause of Christ. If we declare our Christianity through outward displays or external signs but fail to back up what we say with our actions, the world screams, "Hypocrite!"

Once people know we are Christians, they expect to find good fruit emanating from our lives. Jesus says we know a tree by its fruit (Matt. 12:33). He also said that out of the good treasures inside of him, a good man brings forth good things, but an evil man brings forth evil things because what is inside of him is evil (Matt. 12:35). No matter how much a tree may look like an orange tree, if it bears thorns instead of oranges, we know it is not an orange tree. As God's representatives on the earth, the same principle applies to us.

The world is filled with needy people looking for something real and genuine to believe in and be part of. We might say they are hungry, even though they may not realize what they are hungry for. They have a spiritual hunger that nothing can satisfy except an intimate relationship with God, and He wants to use those of us who do believe in Him to reach them. Our lives should be like billboards advertising the beauty of relationship with God through Jesus.

Personal Reflection

Do you have the proper fruit to back up your claim that you are a Christian?

_____

_____

_____

_____

_____

_____

_____

_____

It's easy to go to church and have bumper stickers with Christian phrases or Scriptures on our car, but bearing good fruit is often more difficult. Jeremiah 17:8 says that those who lean on God and put their trust in Him shall be like a tree planted by the water, deeply rooted, that will continue to bear fruit even in drought. No matter what our circumstances are, we should be able to continue bearing good fruit. At the very least, we should be able to see progress as we continue our walk with God. Maybe as baby Christians we bear only a little fruit, but with each year that goes by the harvest of good things radiating from our lives should increase more and more.

Paul specifically mentions in Ephesians 4:1–6 several behaviors we should develop in our lives: humility, gentleness, self-control, patience, unselfish love, and unity. Each of these, as well as others, is very important and should be displayed in our dealings with one another.

Gentleness (Humility, Meekness)

Gentleness often manifests itself in humility and meekness. It is not weakness, as it is often described; it is actually strength under control. Jesus was gentle (meek) and humble (lowly) in heart (Matt. 11:29), yet we know all power was available to Him (Matt. 28:18). He certainly was not weak, but He did use self-control in His dealings with people. When Judas came with a group of men to betray and capture Him, one of Jesus' disciples drew his sword and cut off a man's ear. Jesus told him to put away his sword and reminded him that He could appeal to His Father and He would send twelve legions (armies) of angels to rescue Him if He wanted to. If He did that, however, His Father's will would not have been completed (Matt. 26:49–54). We can see by this that Jesus had power but did not use it, so that a higher purpose could be accomplished. That is true meekness.

Humility manifests in many ways; for example, it is not self-righteous, nor does it judge others critically because of their weaknesses and faults. People who are truly humble never see themselves as better than or superior to others. Self-knowledge helps us develop humility. Knowing ourselves and facing our weaknesses keeps us from feeling superior or judgmental toward other people.

Jesus modeled the type of humility we should seek. He willingly laid aside His divinity and took on humanity (Phil. 2:7). He made Himself a servant. He washed His disciples' feet as an example for them to follow (John 13:1–17). I have also noticed that Jesus never felt the need to defend Himself or prove He was right when others accused Him. Quite often He didn't even answer them. In our relationships with others, it seems we often argue in an effort to prove who is right when we disagree. The truly humble person will realize that it is much better to be humble and kind than to be right. Being right is highly overrated. It gives us a momentary sense of carnal satisfaction, but it does nothing to help us mature spiritually or develop humility.

Paul encourages the Philippian church to let the same attitude and purpose and humble mind that was in Christ Jesus be in them too (Phil. 2:5). This should be our goal also. I think it is safe to say that pride, which is the opposite of humility, is the root of all sin. It certainly is behind selfishness, strife, and many other problems that manifest in our relationships.

Self-control

Displaying the good behaviors Paul teaches us is not always easy, and it requires self-control. Self-control is one fruit of the Holy Spirit that we have inside our human spirit (Gal. 5:22–23). At the time of our new birth in Christ, it is deposited in us along with all the other good fruit God wants us to display. But having this fruit and exercising it are two different things. We may have many things in our possession that we do not use. For example, my phone has a lot of features I don't use often, so when I need them, using them is difficult. The things I do use regularly on my phone—such as text messaging, email, or setting reminders—are easy for me. A similar dynamic happens with good behaviors and the fruit of the Spirit. The more we are called upon to use them, the easier using them becomes.

Patience

As we wait on God to meet our needs and in our dealings with one another, we should be patient. When we are patient we have long-suffering with gentleness and mildness. Patience is not merely waiting for something, but it characterizes how we behave while we wait. The very idea of long-suffering indicates that we will not get what we want quickly. Jesus never allowed His circumstances or unkind people to change how He behaved, and we should not allow them to influence our behavior, either.

People who are patient can deal with difficult situations or people and endure whatever comes with good temper. They continue to display the fruit of love and kindness even during their own personal suffering or unjust treatment. Paul says that we are to bear with one another, which means to make allowances for the weaknesses and faults in others, just as we want them to make allowances for our shortcomings (Col. 3:13). Jesus' instruction to do unto others as we want them do unto us (Matt. 7:12) should be our goal.

We inherit the promises of God through faith and patience (Heb. 6:12), not through faith alone. When we exercise our faith in God, asking Him to do something for us or to change something unpleasant in our lives, we are to wait patiently for Him to do it. These times of waiting test our faith and our patience, and God actually uses them to help us grow spiritually. I believe that being patient with God's timing in our lives as we wait for Him to answer our prayers and fulfill His promises is the foundation of being patient with all other things. The more we use a muscle, the stronger it becomes. Likewise, the more we exercise the good behavior the apostle Paul exhorts us to use, the stronger it becomes.

Unselfish Love

We are to bear with one another in unselfish love. If we only think of what makes us comfortable and of getting our own way all the time, we are selfish, and selfish people are never happy people. The more we walk in love with others, the happier we will be. Paul writes that love is the greatest thing and the most excellent way to live (1 Cor. 12:31). He also writes that love bears all things (regardless of what comes) and that it always believes the best of every person. It remains steadfast during difficult times, and endures everything without becoming weak (1 Cor. 13:7).

Jesus says that we obey His commands if we love Him (John 14:15). One way we can show our love for Him is to show love to others.

Let's be sure we are not like the fig tree, having leaves but no fruit. The only way people can see Jesus through us is for us to behave as He did. People won't always remember what we said to them, but they will remember how we treated them and how we made them feel.

Unity

Paul returns again to encouraging the Ephesians to seek unity and "oneness of the Spirit" (Eph. 4:3). He begins by saying that believers will need to make an effort to do so. Why is unity so hard to maintain? It is simply because we are so diverse and we have different views on many issues and situations.

Our different perspectives often cause division among us, but Paul reminds us that there is one body of believers, one Lord, one hope, one faith, one baptism, and one God and Father of us all. Some reports say that as many as thirty-three thousand different denominations or organizations call themselves "Christian." If that number is even close to being correct, then it is no wonder the influence of the church is not what God intended it to be in society. There are even divisions within denominations and groups.

If two people were stranded on an island and built a church for themselves, it probably would not be long before they would disagree about something and one of them would leave to start another church. All of us are not likely to agree about everything concerning our Christianity, but we should look for the things we do agree on and stop emphasizing so strongly the ones we don't agree on. We must seek unity within diversity. We are all very different. but we can still have unity within our differences if we truly make an effort to do so.

Think about how foolish we would look if we had one head and several different bodies. The Bible teaches us that we Christians are the body of Christ (1 Cor. 12:27). The physical body has many parts and functions, but it is still one unit. Each part of it works together with the others, not against them. Paul uses this analogy to help us understand that God's goal for us as individuals is to work together as one. He may work through each person differently, but we can all still work together remembering that we all serve one Lord.

Satan is the instigator of all strife and division. He knows that the more divided we are, the weaker we become. God says that where there is unity, there will be anointing (the presence and power of God) and blessing (Ps. 133). Each of us must do our part to work toward unity in the church, and one simple way we can begin is by committing to never speak harsh, judgmental words against parts of the body of Christ that are different from ours. True doctrinal error must be confronted in order to prevent people from being deceived, but our personal opinions, likes, and dislikes don't fall into that category. One thing is for sure: when we all get to heaven, there will be perfect unity. There will be no denominations, and we'll likely discover that not one of us had perfect understanding of everything while we were here on earth.

Personal Reflection

How can you grow in expressing humility, gentleness, self-control, patience, unselfish love, and unity in your life?

_____

_____

_____

_____

_____

_____

_____

_____

_____

_____

_____

_____

_____

_____

_____

_____

_____

CHAPTER 8

SPIRITUAL GROWTH AND MATURITY

Growing Spiritually

Ephesians 4:7–10

*Yet grace [God's undeserved favor] was given to each
one of us [not indiscriminately, but in different ways] in
proportion to the measure of Christ's [rich and abundant]
gift. Therefore it says, "WHEN HE ASCENDED ON HIGH, HE
LED CAPTIVITY CAPTIVE, AND HE BESTOWED GIFTS ON MEN."
(Now this expression, "He ascended," what does it mean
except that He also had previously descended [from the
heights of heaven] into the lower parts of the earth? He who
descended is the very same as He who also has ascended
high above all the heavens, that He [His presence] might fill
all things [that is, the whole universe].)*

God has given each of us His grace (ability), but in different
ways. We all have gifts from God and a part to play in His
overall plan. Our goal should be to mature spiritually so we
can do the part God has given us to do while working together
with all the other parts. He has given ministry gifts to help
us in our quest for spiritual growth and maturity. These gifts
were given when Christ ascended on high and led captivity
captive.

H. A. Ironside wrote, "Our blessed Lord in His triumph
over death led captive him who had the power of death up to

that time, that He might deliver those 'who through fear of death were all their lifetime subject to bondage' (Heb. 2:15). In other words, our mighty enemy Satan is now a conquered foe. He has been led captive at the chariot wheels of Christ, and our Lord has now ascended as Man and taken His place upon the throne of the Majesty in the heavens, and there from His exalted seat in glory He gives these gifts to His church for its edification and blessing" (H. A. Ironside, *Ephesians: An Ironside Expository Commentary* [Grand Rapids, MI: Kregel Publications, 1937; repr. 2007], 107).

Our Lord has defeated Satan and stripped him of his power. The only power he now has is what we give him through fear, lack of knowledge, or disobedience. We have the gifts (abilities) we need to carry on the work of Christ. Every person is given the ministry of reconciliation (2 Cor. 5:18). We are to submit to Christ our head and work with Him to see people who are not walking with Him become reconciled to Him.

God Wants to Use Everyone

Ephesians 4:11–13

And [His gifts to the church were varied and] He Himself appointed some as apostles [special messengers, representatives], some as prophets [who speak a new message from God to the people], some as evangelists [who spread the good news of salvation], and some as pastors and teachers [to shepherd and guide and instruct], [and He did this] to fully equip and perfect the saints (God's people) for works of service, to build up the body of Christ [the church]; until we all reach oneness in the faith and in the knowledge of the Son of God, [growing spiritually] to become a mature believer, reaching to the measure of the fullness of Christ [manifesting His spiritual completeness and exercising our spiritual gifts in unity].

God gave us apostles, prophets, evangelists, pastors, and teachers to train others for the work of the ministry. He never intended that these people should do all the work while others become spectators. As a teacher in the body of Christ, my job is to teach and train others concerning what they have in and through Christ and what they should be doing in their daily lives.

Thousands upon thousands of people sit in church week

after week watching someone ministering on a platform, but they leave and do nothing toward serving God in practical ways. They return the next week and the week after and may be proud of their regular church attendance, but they have the mistaken idea that someone else should do all the work of the ministry while they sit idly by and enjoy it. This is not at all what Paul teaches.

Personal Reflection

What are you doing to help someone else? Are you allowing God to use your life to reconcile others to Himself? Are you using the gifts God has given you for the benefit of His Kingdom?

_____

_____

_____

_____

_____

_____

_____

_____

_____

God has given ministry gifts to the church so we will mature spiritually and reach oneness in the faith. We see Paul once again stressing the idea of unity, oneness, and working together for a common cause.

Growing into Maturity as Christians
Ephesians 4:14

So that we are no longer children [spiritually immature],
tossed back and forth [like ships on a stormy sea] and
carried about by every wind of [shifting] doctrine, by
the cunning and trickery of [unscrupulous] men, by the
deceitful scheming of people ready to do anything [for
personal profit].

A full-grown man was not born in that condition. He began as a baby and he grew gradually until he reached maturity. We are the same way as Christians. We begin as spiritual babies. Paul told the Corinthians that he could not feed them the meat of God's Word because although they should have been farther along in their growth, they were still babies in Christ (1 Cor. 3:2). We might say that the milk of the Word or the messages that are easy for us to digest are the ones that teach us what we have from God by His grace, and the meat of the Word are messages that teach us what we should do in light of what God has given us and done for us.

We are to leave the baby stage of Christianity—being concerned mainly with getting our needs met—and gradually grow into spiritual perfection (maturity). In that place of maturity we are not primarily concerned about our own needs but about how we might serve God.

Not one of us has arrived at a place where we no longer need to grow, but we should be able to see that we are growing, changing for the better, and becoming more like Jesus in our behavior. I frequently say, "I am not where I need to be, but thank God, I am not where I used to be." I am growing, and that is what God expects all of us to do.

Things a baby does that may be considered cute when he or she is an infant or a toddler are no longer cute when the person is thirty or forty years old, still doing the same things. For example, small children may ask questions continually, and the parents think their inquisitiveness is cute, but by the time they are fully grown, the parents no longer want to be questioned about every action they take. By then a relationship of trust should have been built between them. A small child may talk too much, and we think it is just part of growing up, but when an adult talks too much and never knows when to listen, it annoys us.

We expect babies to be babies, children to be children, and teenagers to be teenagers, but we also expect adults to behave maturely. Paul writes to the Corinthians that when he was a child he talked like a child, thought like a child, and reasoned like a child, but when he became a man he put aside childish ways (1 Cor. 13:11). If we expect our natural children to do that, surely God expects us to do the same regarding spiritual maturity.

Paul could tell that the Corinthians lacked spiritual maturity because there was still jealousy and strife among them (1 Cor. 3:1–3). In other words, their behavior revealed their level of spiritual maturity. It is no different with us. We can easily locate our level of spiritual maturity by listening to ourselves and examining how we behave, especially under pressure. Paul encourages us to examine ourselves to see if we are behaving as we should (2 Cor. 13:5). I personally think that taking the time to do this on a regular basis is spiritually healthy. It is not to be done so we can feel guilty or condemned when we recognize our faults, but so the Holy Spirit may help us change.

Unless people know who they are in Christ, they cannot do this, because any fault they find or any fault others expose in them immediately makes them feel downcast and condemned. However, when we know that God loves us and never rejects us, we are able to receive correction and actually rejoice in it because we want to be everything God desires us to be.

I would venture to say that it is impossible to reach spiritual maturity without ever receiving correction. We cannot get to where we want to be unless we are honest with ourselves about where we are.

Spiritual children are easily affected emotionally by the storms of life, but Paul wants us to mature so we are no longer manipulated and controlled by our circumstances. Our circumstances may change at any time, but God always remains the same. His Word stands firm, and it will hold us steady in the storms of life if we let it.

Apparently various doctrines came through the church in those days, as they still do today. Paul said the believers would not be deceived by those doctrines or the ones who preached them if they were spiritually mature. People who are mature are sure about what they believe. They are firmly rooted and grounded in God's Word, and nothing and no one can move them from their position. This does not mean that they are never open to learning new things. They are open-minded, but not double-minded.

Growing in Truth as We Continue in God's Word

Ephesians 4:15

But speaking the truth in love [in all things—both our speech and our lives expressing His truth], let us grow up in all things into Him [following His example] who is the Head—Christ.

Modern society tells us that there is no absolute truth. People say truth is relevant to or dependent upon circumstances. In other words, they believe truth can change at any time, but that kind of philosophy is foolish. Truth can only be one thing, and it cannot keep changing. Jesus says that He is Truth (John 14:6), and He is always the same, yesterday, today, and forever (Heb. 13:8). He does not change. We can always depend on Him, and what He says comes to pass.

How can anything be true if there is one truth for me and another truth for someone else? This type of thinking shows us why the world today is a confusing place and in turmoil. Truth is simple. It is what it is and needs no deep introspection to be understood.

Jesus says that if we continue in His Word, we will know the truth and that truth applied to our lives will set us free (John 8:31–32), free from any and all of the things that keep us from enjoying the life Jesus died to give us. Walking in truth will set us free from fear, worry, anxiety, regretting the past, dread, sin, unforgiveness, bitterness, resentment, and many other things.

When we step out on the path of following God, His Word is a light for each step we take (Ps. 119:105), and that path becomes brighter and brighter the more we learn and grow. We study His Word, it reveals truth to us, and that opens our eyes to the deception in which we have been living. Deception happens when lies we believe become our reality because we do not know truth. For example, people who have made many mistakes in their past or have been abused and treated unjustly may believe they can never have a good life, but the truth of God's Word reveals that when we receive Christ as our Savior, we become new men and women; the old things pass away and all things become new (2 Cor. 5:17). We might say our slate is wiped clean and we get a fresh start.

We should love the truth and speak the truth in love in all things, letting both our speech and our conduct express God's truth. As we do, we will grow up and become spiritually mature.

Properly Joined Together

Ephesians 4:16

*From Him the whole body [the church, in all its various
parts], joined and knitted firmly together by what every
joint supplies, when each part is working properly,
causes the body to grow and mature, building itself up in
[unselfish] love.*

Paul ends this section of his letter with another encouragement to be joined together with other believers so the body
of Christ can work properly. As we come together and apply
our Christian principles in our dealings with one another,
we grow spiritually. When someone offends us, we learn to
quickly forgive. When we notice the flaws and weaknesses of
another person, we bear with that person, keeping an eye on
ourselves so we will not also be tempted (Gal. 6:1). We might
say that we practice our Christianity on each other.

If we merely have an abstract view of Christianity in which
we gain knowledge, but we are never in situations where we
are called upon to apply what we have learned, we do not
grow. What we think we know is never solidified because we
never demonstrate it. But in relationship with one another we
must regularly apply what we have learned, and when we do,
the entire body of Christians benefits. If a believer in Christ

only relates to people of the world who do not care how he behaves, he will never be called to account for his actions. But when we are with people who are like-minded with us, we will be called upon to behave properly. Unless people are truly ready for a full commitment to Christ and desire spiritual maturity, they will usually avoid those who hold them accountable for their behavior.

Paul writes frequently about carnality or carnal Christians, meaning people who have been saved by grace but have not matured and still walk according to the flesh. They follow ordinary impulses and the thoughts of their own minds. We are called to something much higher than that. We are called to grow into spiritual maturity, becoming like Christ in all our ways.

Personal Reflection

Do you have friends and family in your life who keep you accountable and who will confront you if you behave in a way that is not pleasing to God?

_____

_____

_____

_____

_____

CHAPTER 9

—◆—

THE CHRISTIAN'S JOURNEY

Live Like a Believer

Ephesians 4:17–21

So this I say, and solemnly affirm together with the Lord
[as in His presence], that you must no longer live as the
[unbelieving] Gentiles live, in the futility of their minds [and
in the foolishness and emptiness of their souls], for their
[moral] understanding is darkened and their reasoning is
clouded; [they are] alienated and self-banished from the life
of God [with no share in it; this is] because of the [willful]
ignorance and spiritual blindness that is [deep-seated]
within them, because of the hardness and insensitivity
of their heart. And they, [the ungodly in their spiritual
apathy], having become callous and unfeeling, have given
themselves over [as prey] to unbridled sensuality, eagerly
craving the practice of every kind of impurity [that their
desires may demand]. But you did not learn Christ in this
way! If in fact you have [really] heard Him and have been
taught by Him, just as truth is in Jesus [revealed in His life
and personified in Him].

The apostle Paul frequently teaches the same message in a
variety of ways. He tells the Philippians that to write the same
things to them again is no trouble for him, and is a safeguard
for them (Phil. 3:1). Paul affirms to the Ephesians the great

importance of their behavior and reminds them that they must not live as the unbelieving Gentiles do.

We should never feel it is boring or useless to hear things repeated because we easily and quickly forget what we have heard. Satan works very hard to distract us. He especially wants to distract us after we hear or study God's Word. The apostle Mark says that he comes immediately and tries to take away what was sown into our hearts (Mark 4:15). Satan does not want us to meditate on it as the Bible instructs us to do. He wants us to forget it quickly so it does not take root in our hearts and start producing good fruit. You could read this book ten times, and each time you might very well learn something you missed previously or at least be reminded of some very important truths and principles God doesn't want you to forget.

We live in the world, and we have a tendency to pick up the habits of other people if we are around them often, so Paul wants to make plain the condition of the unbelievers. They have no relationship with God and do not know Him. They live in the vanity (uselessness) of their minds. They follow their own thoughts and emotions and do as they please. They live according to their own reasoning, but they are deceived. They don't have the life of God in them, as Christians do. Their hearts have been hardened by sin, and they practice every kind of impurity. Considering these things, it would be foolish to follow their example. The psalmist David says that we should not take counsel from the ungodly (Ps. 1:1).

We might wonder how a person could choose to live that

kind of seemingly miserable life, yet multitudes do. I have noticed that unbelievers often find fault with others, and especially with Christians. This gives them an excuse to ignore their own behavior. I knew a very wicked man who continually criticized and judged other people, even though his behavior was much worse than theirs. He scrutinized the lives of any Christians he knew and was quick to magnify any mistakes they might make. He frequently said, "They go to church, but they are no better than I am."

Paul reminds the believers that they are not to behave as the unbelievers do, for they have been taught better than that. The more unbelievers we are around, at work or even in the family, the more we need to be reminded not to follow their example but instead to be an example to them. As we let them see our godly behavior, our peace and joy, hopefully it will reveal to them that there is a better way to live than they are currently living.

Put on the New Self

Ephesians 4:22–24

... That, regarding your previous way of life, you put off your old self [completely discard your former nature], which is being corrupted through deceitful desires, and be continually renewed in the spirit of your mind [having a fresh, untarnished mental and spiritual attitude], and put on the new self [the regenerated and renewed nature], created in God's image, [godlike] in the righteousness and holiness of the truth [living in a way that expresses to God your gratitude for your salvation].

When we are born again (receive Christ as our Savior) we are given a new nature and a new heart. Although we have been made new, Paul says that we must daily put on the new self. He means we must choose over and over again to do what we know to be right. We are to completely discard our old way of life, because to be a new creature in Christ and continue in old ways would be tragic.

In verse 22 Paul says we are to put off the old self, or walk away from old ways, and in verse 24 he says that we are to put on the new self that has been re-created in God's image. That sounds simple enough, but we find in our experience that we often fail. I have found verse 23 to be very helpful, and I call it the bridge Scripture between verses 22 and 24. If we want to put off the old self and put on the new self, we need to continually be renewed in our minds. This happens as we spend time studying God's Word and meditating on His principles. We are to have a fresh mental and spiritual attitude daily. Our thoughts always precede our actions; therefore, we need to think new thoughts in order to behave according to the new self.

It is very important for us to understand these three verses. We are made new in Christ, but the old nature still tries to rule us. We must say no to it as often as needed, and that could be multiple times each day. We don't receive Christ and then find we are never tempted after that. Our Christian journey is a daily walk, and each good decision we make is another step closer to experiencing the good life God has made ready for us.

You need not feel guilty if you are tempted, because temptation comes to all of us. Just ask the Holy Spirit to make you quickly aware of Satan's strategies and say no to him when he tempts you to do what is wrong.

Behavior to Avoid

Ephesians 4:25–28

Therefore, rejecting all falsehood [whether lying, defrauding, telling half-truths, spreading rumors, any such as these], SPEAK TRUTH EACH ONE WITH HIS NEIGHBOR, for we are all parts of one another [and we are all parts of the body of Christ]. BE ANGRY [at sin—at immorality, at injustice, at ungodly behavior], YET DO NOT SIN; do not let your anger [cause you shame, nor allow it to] last until the sun goes down. And do not give the devil an opportunity [to lead you into sin by holding a grudge, or nurturing anger, or harboring resentment, or cultivating bitterness]. The thief [who has become a believer] must no longer steal, but instead he must work hard [making an honest living], producing that which is good with his own hands, so that he will have something to share with those in need.

Paul mentions specific behaviors Christians are to avoid. We are to walk in truth, as he previously taught us. It is our job to reject falsehood, whether it comes in the form of lies, half-truths, or rumors. Satan is a liar, and he delights in telling us lies either through other people or by putting into our minds thoughts that are not truthful according to God's Word.

In addition, we are not to be angry and let it drag us into

sin. Anger is an emotion we all experience, and, among other things, it lets us know if we are being unjustly treated. If someone is rude to us we may immediately feel angry, but we have the ability to control what we choose to do at that point. We can act on the anger and say or do things that are not pleasing to God, or we can trust God to deal with those who have injured us, rather than trying to take revenge on them. Being quick to forgive is the antidote for anger. I often tell people, "Do yourself a favor: forgive." When we forgive we release those who have injured us into the hands of God, and we trust Him to deal with them in a way that will bring them into the truth.

Paul instructs us not to let our anger last until the sun goes down. Working through the emotion of anger often takes time, and Paul seems to understand that. We should not sleep on our anger, because what we go to bed with at night, we will wake up with the next day. Those thoughts and feelings have all night to take root in our souls, and the longer they remain, the more difficult they may be to get rid of. The more quickly we do the right thing, the easier it is to do it.

When we stay angry and allow it to lead us into sin, we open a door for the devil. We give him an opportunity to lead us into more and more sin as we nurture our anger. Two wrongs never make a right. When someone treats us wrong and then we have a wrong response, it is never the answer to the problem. We have been given a new way of living, and we must repeatedly choose to do what is right no matter how we may feel about it. When we choose to do what is right while it is difficult or seems unfair, that is when we grow spiritually. Every right choice is another step in our journey of spiritual maturity.

Paul reminds us to turn our backs on our old life. For example, if someone was once a thief, that person is to steal no more. Selfishness may urge a thief to steal, but now Paul says that individual is to work hard at something that is honest so he has something to share with others. He doesn't even tell him to work hard only in order to take care of himself, but directs his attention to a new goal. He directs his readers away from selfishness to sharing with others. The sinful life is the selfish life; it is filled with selfish thoughts and ways, but we overcome evil with good (Rom. 12:21). The new person in Christ doesn't even need to focus on trying to stop doing the wrong thing if he focuses on doing the right thing. Do what is right, and you will have no room in your life for doing what is wrong. If we make new habits, there will be no room for the old ones.

Don't Grieve the Holy Spirit

Ephesians 4:29–32

*Do not let unwholesome [foul, profane, worthless, vulgar]
words ever come out of your mouth, but only such* speech
as is good for building up others, according to the need and
*the occasion, so that it will be a blessing to those who hear
[you speak]. And do not grieve the Holy Spirit of God [but
seek to please Him], by whom you were sealed* and marked
*[branded as God's own] for the day of redemption [the final
deliverance from the consequences of sin]. Let all bitterness
and wrath and anger and clamor [perpetual animosity,
resentment, strife, fault-finding] and slander be put away
from you, along with every kind of malice [all spitefulness,
verbal abuse, malevolence]. Be kind* and *helpful to one
another, tender-hearted [compassionate, understanding],
forgiving one another [readily and freely], just as God in
Christ also forgave you.*

Now we come to a subject that I feel very passionate about
because I believe it is extremely important: the words we
speak. With God's help, we are to exercise discipline and
self-control and not allow anything foul or worthless to come
out of our mouths. We are to speak words that build up and
encourage others. Once again I encourage you to focus on

saying the right things, and then there will be no room for the wrong things. No one can tame the tongue without God's help, according to James 3:6, 8, because the tongue is an unruly evil that is set on fire by hell.

Satan is the one who provokes us to speak useless and damaging words. He does so in order for our words to wound others, but they also wound us. Other people are not the only ones who hear the words we speak; we hear them too. You have surely heard the phrase "You are going to eat those words," but what was its origin? I believe it originated with Scripture: "Death and life are in the power of the tongue, and those who love it and indulge it will eat its fruit and bear the consequences of their words" (Prov. 18:21).

Words are tiny containers for power, but we can choose whether they will be filled with negative, harmful power, or with positive, energizing, uplifting power. Choosing our words carefully is most important because once words have left our mouths and gone out into the atmosphere, we cannot get them back. They are working either for or against us, as well as in the lives of other people. We can, of course, repent for any wrong words we have spoken, but they may have already done their damage. I can apologize to someone I have wounded, but harmful words often stick with a person and continue to do their evil work.

It is sobering indeed to realize that our wrong words grieve and sadden the Holy Spirit of God. He is the one who is keeping us safe until our time on earth has ended and we are fully delivered from the consequences of sin. His ministry to us in our daily life helps us as we learn to walk with God. The thoughts of grieving the Holy Spirit should make us take seriously this issue concerning our words.

I believe that when we grieve the Holy Spirit, we will also feel grieved because He lives in us; however, we might not connect feelings of sadness or even depression to our words. Most often when we have problems, we look for someone or something to blame, but sometimes *we* are the source of our own trouble. The next time you feel sad, depressed, or as though you are grieving in your spirit, think about what you have been thinking about and talking about. Wrong thoughts and unwholesome, worthless words may not be the root of the problem, but they are worth examining.

There are other things that also grieve the Holy Spirit, including bitterness, anger, resentment, strife, fault-finding, and slander. These are practices Christians should avoid, but sadly, that is not always the case. Far too many angry Christians have repeatedly heard messages about forgiving those who hurt them, but they have yet to be obedient and do it.

There is an abundance of gossip, fault-finding, strife, and slander in the world, but it is also in our churches—and they are the last places on earth we should encounter that kind of behavior. We would expect to see such sins among unbelievers, but we should not find them among God's children. Paul says we should put them away from us and choose to be kind and helpful to one another, forgiving others as readily and freely as God has forgiven us.

Let's take this matter of not grieving the Holy Spirit very

seriously, for it seems to me to be a very serious thing. I find it interesting that of all the sins a person might commit, those concerning how we treat one another seem extremely important to God. He loves people, and He wants us to love them on His behalf. We need to show love and make people feel valued. Many times when we say something kind to another person, they will reply, "You just made my day!" That shows how desperate people are to hear uplifting, encouraging words. You can learn more about this in my book *Change Your Words, Change Your Life*.

The Holy Spirit is an encourager, and He works to bring hope and healing to wounded souls. We should work with Him, not against Him. When the prophet Isaiah entered the presence of God, he said that he was ruined because he realized he was a man of unclean lips (Is. 6:4–5). Then an angel touched his mouth, his sins were forgiven, and God used him mightily (Is. 6:6–7). Let us offer our mouths to God for His use.

I am grateful for the teaching of the prophets and apostles on this subject, which is found throughout the Word of God. I pray for myself and for you that we will not grieve the Holy Spirit with our words and actions.

CHAPTER 10

LIVING A CHRISTLIKE LIFE

Be Imitators of God
Ephesians 5:1–2

Therefore become imitators of God [copy Him and follow His example], as well-beloved children [imitate their father]; and walk continually in love [that is, value one another— practice empathy and compassion, unselfishly seeking the best for others], just as Christ also loved you and gave Himself up for us, an offering and sacrifice to God [slain for you, so that it became] a sweet fragrance.

Anytime someone tells a father that his child looks like him or acts like him, it gives him joy. I am sure our Father in heaven feels the same way. Paul is calling us to the highest standard in the world when he says we are to be imitators of God. We should imitate Him in conduct, purity of thought, speech, and holiness in all of our ways. Living to please God is one way we can show our love and appreciation for Him and for all He has done for us.

God wants us to love as He loves and to forgive as He forgives. The quality of love Paul writes about requires sacrifice. Just as Jesus sacrificed Himself for us, we are to sacrifice ourselves for others. We may be called upon to do things we don't want to do for others or to forgive someone who has abused or treated us unjustly. Love can be costly. It may cost time,

money, effort, or being patient with someone who is difficult to deal with. Everyone God asks us to love is not easy to
love, but if we are willing to do it as a sacrifice to God, He is
pleased.

In biblical times, when sacrifices were offered to a god on
an altar, they produced a sweet smell that supposedly went up
and pleased the god for whom they were intended. Paul told
the Ephesians they were to love and forgive others just as God
had loved and forgiven them and that their doing so would be
a sacrifice to God, whom they were now serving.

The Importance of Avoiding Immorality

Ephesians 5:3–7

But sexual immorality and all [moral] impurity [indecent, offensive behavior] or greed must not even be hinted at among you, as is proper among saints [for as believers our way of life, whether in public or in private, reflects the validity of our faith]. Let there be no filthiness and silly talk, or coarse [obscene or vulgar] joking, because such things are not appropriate [for believers]; but instead speak of your thankfulness [to God]. For be sure of this: no immoral, impure, or greedy person—for that one is [in effect] an idolater—has any inheritance in the kingdom of Christ and God [for such a person places a higher value on something other than God]. Let no one deceive you with empty arguments [that encourage you to sin], for because of these things the wrath of God comes upon the sons of disobedience [those who habitually sin]. So do not participate or even associate with them [in the rebelliousness of sin].

Paul lists behaviors that should be avoided, and sexual immorality is on the top of the list. Chastity was unheard of in those days. The very idea of expecting a young man to avoid sex would have been considered extremely severe and ridiculous. Men normally had a mistress, and there were even temples that had priestesses who were prostitutes and whose earnings paid for the upkeep of the temple.

One such place was built to Aphrodite, who was considered the goddess of love. The Greeks were the first to introduce prostitution as a profitable business, and brothels were opened in Athens. Understanding the culture of these people to whom Paul wrote and introduced this message about sexual purity helps us grasp why he repeated it often. He told the Corinthians to flee from sexual impurity (1 Cor. 6:18). He told the Colossians to put sexual immorality to death (Col. 3:5). He told the Galatians it was a work of the flesh, and he warned them to stay away from it (Gal. 5:16–21).

In Paul's day corruption and immorality of all kinds were everywhere. We might say that Christ started a moral revolution that was nothing less than a miracle. Paul said that immoral behavior of any kind, whether it is indecent sexual behavior, greed, or coarse and vulgar language, is not appropriate for the Christian. The New King James Bible translation says that it should not even be "named among" believers. Paul said those who practiced these sins had no inheritance in the Kingdom of God. This does not apply to someone who is born again and who sins and is repentant, but to those who perpetually practice sinning and are unrepentant. It is important to realize that God has called us out of an ungodly and immoral lifestyle into a godly, holy, and moral one. Christians are to hate sin and do all we can to live holy lives.

Deception was widespread in Paul's day, just as it is today, and Paul urged the Ephesians not to let anyone deceive them with empty arguments. One such deception was called Gnosticism, and it taught that only the spirit is good and all matter is evil. To the Gnostics, only the spirit had value and all other matter, including a person's body, was without importance. Some of the Gnostics concluded and taught that because of this belief, what people did with their bodies did not matter. They could feel free to act on any physical desire they had, no matter how impure it was. Christianity, however, is concerned with the salvation and sanctification of the whole person—spirit, soul, and body (1 Thess. 5:23). Paul said we were bought with a price, and therefore we should glorify God with our bodies (1 Cor. 6:20). The precious blood of Jesus was the price God paid to purchase us.

Although the deception of Gnosticism came from outside the church, there were also people within the church who spread deception by perverting the grace of God. They believed they should sin so that God's grace could abound. However, Paul confronted this deceptive idea by clearly stating how foolish it was (Rom. 6:1–2). As I noted earlier, grace is God's undeserved favor, but it is also the power of God that enables us to live holy lives. Grace is an amazing and wonderful gift, but it also comes with responsibility. God's grace forgives our sin, but we are still obligated to live the best way we can, and we have a responsibility to do so.

I was once asked if someone could be actively involved in criminal activity and have God continue to bless and prosper him because he was covered by grace. The question grieved me, and I was astonished that anyone could ask such a thing.

But that is what deception does to a person's mind if it is not confronted. People are gradually sucked into a type of error that can lead them to do things that are totally unreasonable, yet they will continue to think there is nothing wrong with their behavior. We should all pray that we will not be deceived (Matt. 24:4).

Paul said that we should not participate or even associate with people who practice the kind of immorality he has addressed. We cannot avoid everyone in the world involved in evil, otherwise we would have to get out of the world, but we are not to associate closely with them and perhaps learn their ways (1 Cor. 5:9–11).

I believe people living in sin need the influence and example of godly Christians, so I don't suggest avoiding them altogether. When we associate with them, we need to be sure we are influencing them for good, not allowing them to infect us with sinful and deceptive ideas.

Personal Reflection

Do you have friends who are not a good influence on you?

_____

_____

_____

_____

_____

Living in the Light

Ephesians 5:8–13

For once you were darkness, but now you are light in the Lord; walk as children of Light [live as those who are native-born to the Light] (for the fruit [the effect, the result] of the Light consists in all goodness and righteousness and truth), trying to learn [by experience] what is pleasing to the Lord [and letting your lifestyles be examples of what is most acceptable to Him—your behavior expressing gratitude to God for your salvation]. Do not participate in the worthless and unproductive deeds of darkness, but instead expose them [by exemplifying personal integrity, moral courage, and godly character]; for it is disgraceful even to mention the things that such people practice in secret. But all things become visible when they are exposed by the light [of God's precepts], for it is light that makes everything visible.

Paul reminds the believing Gentiles that although they were once filled with darkness and participated in all these evil practices, they are now new creations filled with light and called to walk in the light. Jesus is the light (John 8:12).

The light is full of goodness and the truth of God's Word. When light floods a dark place, things once hidden are exposed. As we walk in the light of God's truth, evil things are exposed and we see things differently than we did previously. Doing what is right becomes our primary concern, and we should seek to please God in all things. We all make mistakes and we make them often, but if our heart's attitude is to do right, God works with us and we are gradually changed more and more into the image of Christ (2 Cor. 3:18).

We can learn by our experience what is pleasing to God and what isn't. We have the Holy Spirit living inside of us, and He reveals sin to us, helping us know what we should and should not do. One way He does this is by making us a little uncomfortable about what we are doing if it is not right. If we persist in wrong behavior, our ability to experience the Lord's peace and joy will decrease. God's Word says we are to follow peace, and if peace is not present, it is wise to reexamine our actions (Col. 3:15; Heb. 12:14).

I love the ministry of the Holy Spirit in my life because it is a safeguard for me. He points out sin in our lives as well as in the lives of others, and that keeps us safe, as long as we listen to Him. The moment the Holy Spirit shows us sin of any kind, we are to turn away from it and choose to live a lifestyle that is pleasing to God.

Personal Reflection

Are you currently doing anything you don't have peace about doing?

_____

_____

_____

_____

_____

_____

_____

_____

_____

_____

_____

_____

_____

_____

_____

_____

_____

_____

Living Carefully

Ephesians 5:14–21

For this reason He says, "Awake, sleeper, and arise from the dead, and Christ will shine [as dawn] upon you and give you light." Therefore see that you walk carefully [living life with honor, purpose, and courage; shunning those who tolerate and enable evil], not as the unwise, but as wise [sensible, intelligent, discerning people], making the very most of your time [on earth, recognizing and taking advantage of each opportunity and using it with wisdom and diligence], because the days are [filled with] evil. Therefore do not be foolish and thoughtless, but understand and firmly grasp what the will of the Lord is. Do not get drunk with wine, for that is wickedness (corruption, stupidity), but be filled with the [Holy] Spirit and constantly guided by Him. Speak to one another in psalms and hymns and spiritual songs, [offering praise by] singing and making melody with your heart to the Lord; always giving thanks to God the Father for all things, in the name of our Lord Jesus Christ; being subject to one another out of reverence for Christ.

In these verses Paul talks about a very important issue— making the most of our time. We are to seize each day and live with purpose, not being foolish and living as one who is unwise. I wrote an entire book on this subject, called *Seize the Day*, because it is easy to waste not only time but an entire life.

Young people often feel that they have all the time in the world. I remember taking time for granted for years until I realized I had already lived at least two-thirds of my life, and at that point I became more serious than ever about making sure I didn't waste any time. Not wasting time doesn't mean we should fill every second with activity, but it does mean we should give forethought to what we do with our time and use it wisely. We are not to be what I call "sleepy Christians," but to be alert and watchful, and to live carefully and with purpose.

Paul tells us to seize every opportunity to do good because the days are evil. We are to understand and firmly grasp the will of God and do all we possibly can to walk in it. Let me encourage you not to waste another day being angry for any reason. Don't waste time being jealous, greedy, living in sin, or being miserable. Shake off all darkness, and walk fully in God's light, letting the Holy Spirit lead you into the best life you can possibly have.

It saddens me deeply to see an elderly person who is close to death realize that they wasted their entire life and have nothing left but regrets. I am sure we all know such people, but let us strive to make sure this does not happen to us.

Greek culture included pagan gatherings called symposiums. These gatherings were drinking parties where people ate, sang songs, discussed various topics, and got drunk. Paul tells his readers that when they gather together, they are not to engage in such behavior, but to be filled with the Holy Spirit, sing songs to the Lord, be thankful, and have conversations filled with good things. It is possible that many of the people Paul was talking to had attended and enjoyed these parties. Perhaps they would miss going to them, but Paul wants them to know that God is inviting them to gather in a different way, a way that will be rewarding and not a waste of time. God wants us to enjoy ourselves but to do so in ways that are good and beneficial to us.

Getting drunk is certainly a waste of time, and it usually leaves one feeling sick and miserable. But being filled with the Holy Spirit while being occupied in godly activity not only is enjoyable, but its benefits are long lasting. Choose wisely what you do with your time.

When people talk about not having enough time, they frequently say they cannot find time to study the Bible, pray, or spend time with God. The truth is that we spend our time doing whatever is most important to us. When God is first in our lives, we put Him first in our time, and then He enables us to accomplish all the other things we should be doing. One thing is for sure: most people are very busy these days. But God has not called us just to be busy, but to be fruitful. We can be busy from daybreak until bedtime every day yet not bear any good fruit simply because what we are doing is useless and a waste of time.

We need rest, work, play, worship, and entertainment to live well-balanced lives, but we should be able to look at our life as a whole and say, "I believe I am in the will of God, and I think I am fulfilling my purpose and not wasting my life."

God has given us free will, and a certain amount of time is allotted to each of us during our lifetime. What we do with that time is our choice. Free will is a huge responsibility as well as a privilege. Our choices say a lot about us and about our character. Each day is a gift from God, and we have the opportunity to value it or to waste it. We often live as if there is no tomorrow, and yet tomorrow always comes. If we are not satisfied with today, perhaps it is due to making bad choices yesterday. We can always recover from bad choices by beginning immediately to make good ones.

God wants us to live *on* purpose *for* a purpose, and there is no time like the present to get started if you haven't already.

Personal Reflection

Do you feel that you use most of your time wisely, or do you get to the end of too many days and wonder why you didn't accomplish what you truly wanted to do?

_____

_____

_____

_____

_____

_____

_____

CHAPTER 11

THE CHRISTIAN FAMILY AND RELATING TO AUTHORITY

Christian Marriage
Ephesians 5:22–33

Wives, be subject to your own husbands, as [a service] to the Lord. For the husband is head of the wife, as Christ is head of the church, Himself being the Savior of the body. But as the church is subject to Christ, so also wives should be subject to their husbands in everything [respecting both their position as protector and their responsibility to God as head of the house]. Husbands, love your wives [seek the highest good for her and surround her with a caring, unselfish love], just as Christ also loved the church and gave Himself up for her, so that He might sanctify the church, having cleansed her by the washing of water with the word [of God], so that [in turn] He might present the church to Himself in glorious splendor, without spot or wrinkle or any such thing; but that she would be holy [set apart for God] and blameless. Even so husbands should and are morally obligated to love their own wives as [being in a sense] their own bodies. He who loves his own wife loves himself. For no one ever hated his own body, but [instead] he nourishes and protects and cherishes it, just as Christ does the church, because we are members (parts) of His body. FOR THIS REASON A MAN SHALL LEAVE HIS FATHER AND HIS MOTHER AND SHALL BE JOINED [and be faithfully devoted] TO HIS WIFE, AND THE TWO SHALL BECOME ONE FLESH. This

*mystery [of two becoming one] is great; but I am speaking
with reference to [the relationship of] Christ and the church.
However, each man among you [without exception] is to
love his wife as his very own self [with behavior worthy of
respect and esteem, always seeking the best for her with an
attitude of lovingkindness], and the wife [must see to it] that
she respects and delights in her husband [that she notices
him and prefers him and treats him with loving concern,
treasuring him, honoring him, and holding him dear].*

Now Paul turns his attention to the Christian family and to
how each individual member should function with the others. He begins by stating that we are to submit to one another
out of reverence for Christ. That one sentence sets the tone for
the remainder of what he wants to say.

At this point in our study of Ephesians, we approach a subject that has been abused in the past. A wife is to submit to
her husband and do it as a service to the Lord, for he is the
head of the wife and of the entire family, even as Christ is the
head of the church.

Let's look at the cultural situation that existed as Paul
wrote this letter. Jewish men had a low view of women. History teaches us that part of a Jewish man's morning prayer
was "God, thank You that I am not a Gentile, a slave, or a
woman." In Paul's day, women had no rights and were the
absolute possessions of their husbands. Because of things
like this, women were often mistreated and taken advantage

of. I'm sure that Paul's instruction for women to submit to their husbands was met with some hesitation and frustration, even as it is today. But Paul's message is very balanced, and he writes to men as well as women.

God asks women to submit to the leadership and guidance of their husbands, but the husbands also have a responsibility to love their wives in the same way that Christ loves the church. It is amazing that God compares the relationship of the husband and wife to the relationship of Jesus to the church.

A husband is to nurture his wife, seek her highest good, and love her as he loves his own body. This type of love would eliminate all selfishness. In Genesis 2:24 we are taught that when husband and wife are joined, they become one flesh. Paul said this mystery of the two becoming one is very great, and he compares it to Christ's relationship with the church.

The footnote on verse 22 in the Amplified Bible says, "The wife should submit to her husband, not to men in general, not as inferior to him, nor in violation of her Christian ethics, but honoring her husband as protector and head of the home, respecting the responsibility of his position and his account-ability to God."

As we know, this idea of a woman submitting to her husband is not very popular today, and there are many reasons for that. What Paul describes is a seemingly perfect situation, and we can easily see how beautiful it would be and how willingly the two would enter into it fully. However, we are far from that type of perfection, and a great deal of rebellion on the part of women as well as abuse toward women from their husbands has soured this ideal.

A Christian woman will want to obey God in this area, and she should make every effort to do so, remembering that she is never called upon to submit to anything that wars against her conscience or Christian principles. Men have an equal responsibility, and Paul lays it out clearly. The question becomes, "What am I supposed to do if I am willing to do my part but my spouse does not do theirs?" Should a woman submit to her husband if he is selfish and thinks only of himself, not honoring and nurturing her? Or, should the husband love his wife as his own body and give himself up for her if she does not respect and honor his authority?

One person's wrongdoing never eliminates another person's responsibility to do what is right. Each one is responsible before God to live to please Him and should try their utmost to do so. Many different types of situations occur within the marriage relationship, and I cannot comment in this book on everything a wife or husband might encounter. I do, however, encourage each one to do their best in this area and do it unto the Lord, as a service to Him. I trust that God will give guidance to each person in their specific situations.

The main thing to remember is that God wants order and peace in the home. If peace is missing, we are to seek God about what we need to do in order to see it restored.

Personal Reflection

Do you have peace in your home, and are you doing your part to be obedient to the instructions in Ephesians 5 regarding the marriage relationship?

_____

_____

_____

_____

_____

_____

_____

_____

_____

_____

_____

_____

_____

_____

_____

_____

_____

_____

Parents and Children

Ephesians 6:1–4

Children, obey your parents in the Lord [that is, accept their guidance and discipline as His representatives], for this is right [for obedience teaches wisdom and self-discipline]. HONOR *[esteem, value as precious]* YOUR FATHER AND YOUR MOTHER *[and be respectful to them]—this is the first commandment with a promise—*SO THAT IT MAY BE WELL WITH YOU, AND THAT YOU MAY HAVE A LONG LIFE ON THE EARTH. *Fathers, do not provoke your children to anger [do not exasperate them to the point of resentment with demands that are trivial or unreasonable or humiliating or abusive; nor by showing favoritism or indifference to any of them], but bring them up [tenderly, with lovingkindness] in the discipline and instruction of the Lord.*

Ephesians 6 may be best known as the chapter that includes Paul's powerful message about putting on the armor of God in order to deal with the devil. Before that, though, he continues his instructions on family relationships, which he began in chapter 5 when discussing the relationship between husband and wife. Now he turns his attention to children and parents, and we find once again that his instructions are to both parties in the relationship. Children are to obey and respect their parents because it is the right thing to do. In fact, it is part of the Ten Commandments that God gave to Moses (Exod. 20:12). It is the first command with a promise—that things will go well with the children, and they will have a long life if they honor their parents.

Not everyone has had good experiences with their parents, and honoring fathers and mothers can be difficult for some people. That does not excuse anyone from obeying this Scripture. When honoring parents is challenging, it's important for people to relate to their parents as best they can, based on love for God and respect for His Word.

I can use my relationship with my own parents as an example. They had abused me all the years I was growing up, but as they entered their senior years they needed to be cared for, and I knew in my heart that God wanted me to take on that responsibility. Honoring them by caring for them wasn't something I wanted to do or was excited about doing, but I knew it was the right thing to do. I did it because of my love and respect for God.

Fathers (parents) have equal responsibility and are not to provoke their children to anger or cause resentment by making unreasonable demands. Today we often see rebellion among young people in school as well as at home, but we also see many parents who are not living the lifestyle they should live in order to be good examples to their children. In other words, they are not living in ways that inspire their children to respect them.

The apostle James writes that strife (contention, selfish

ambition, and jealousy) causes rebellion "and every evil thing" (James 3:16). Just think about how many homes today are frequently filled with strife, arguing, bickering, and heated disagreements. This is not the atmosphere that produces submissive children. Our children need to have a stable atmosphere in which to grow up, and they need to be taught strong moral principles from the time they are very young. Parents teach children not only with their words but also with their actions, so it is very important for children to see good examples in their parents on a regular basis.

I urge parents to make every effort to provide a godly, loving, and peaceful atmosphere for their children to grow up in. If children don't see this kind of good example at home, they may never see it anywhere else.

I think we can say that the home is the foundation for all other things, so the proper order for family relationships must begin at home. If great damage has already been done to a parent-child relationship, it is not too late to make amends and begin again. It may take some time and effort, but it will be worth doing, because nothing is more enjoyable than good relationships, especially within a family.

Relating to Authority

Ephesians 6:5–9

Slaves, be obedient to those who are your earthly masters, with respect for authority, and with a sincere heart [seeking to please them], as [service] to Christ—not in the way of eye-service [working only when someone is watching you and only] to please men, but as slaves of Christ, doing the will of God from your heart; rendering service with goodwill, as to the Lord, and not [only] to men, knowing that whatever good thing each one does, he will receive this back from the Lord, whether [he is] slave or free. You masters, do the same [showing goodwill] toward them, and give up threatening and abusive words, knowing that [He who is] both their true Master and yours is in heaven, and that there is no partiality with Him [regardless of one's earthly status].

Paul goes on to tell slaves that they should be obedient to their masters and respect their authority. I read that at one time there were approximately 60 million slaves in the Roman Empire. Many were captured during wartime, some were criminals, and some were born into bondage. Others were indentured, which meant they were in debt and had no way to pay what they owed except to work for the person who redeemed them from their debts.

Not all slaves were mistreated. Many held high household positions and became trusted friends to the master of the home. It was not uncommon for them to be given their freedom and then choose to remain in service because of their love and respect for their masters. In those days people were bought and sold legally in public settings. Thankfully, the vile practice as it took place in Paul's day has been discontinued. Nevertheless, we can all benefit from these instructions because most of us either work for an employer or employ others to work for us. We sell our labor and someone buys it, but each party has a responsibility to treat the other with proper respect.

Paul told the masters (employers) to treat those who worked for them with dignity and kindness. Paul's letter reminds both parties that they are responsible to the Lord and should live to please Him. The worker should work unto the Lord and not just to please other people. The employer should remember that with God there is no favoritism (Rom. 2:11) but that He is good to all. People in authority who misuse or abuse those under their authority will answer to God for their actions.

We all represent Christ in our work as well as in our homes, and we should conduct ourselves according to Christian principles. In the workplace we often have opportunities to be witnesses for Christ, so it is imperative that our attitudes be appropriate for Christian workers or Christian employers.

It is not simply those in authority who deserve respect; every person deserves it. Each of us is valuable to God, and we have a purpose on earth. No one should be devalued or treated in a way that makes them feel that they have no worth.

The workplace provides ample opportunity to show God's love on a continual basis. We may work with people who are hurting because of things that have happened to them, or because they are ill or in physical pain, or because they are lonely. What they need is a touch from God, and it can come through us. Let me encourage you to put on Christ daily as you go to work and remember that, in reality, He is the one you are working for. Whether you are an employee or an employer, your reward will come from Him.

Personal Reflection

If you are an employer, do you treat all your employees according to Paul's godly instructions? If you are an employee, do you go to work daily with a Christian attitude, ready to work hard and be respectful to those in authority as a service to the Lord?

_____

_____

_____

_____

_____

CHAPTER 12

SPIRITUAL WARFARE AND THE VICTORIOUS CHRISTIAN LIFE

Dealing Effectively with the Devil
Ephesians 6:10–17

In conclusion, be strong in the Lord [draw your strength from Him and be empowered through your union with Him] and in the power of His [boundless] might. Put on the full armor of God [for His precepts are like the splendid armor of a heavily-armed soldier], so that you may be able to [successfully] stand up against all the schemes and the strategies and the deceits of the devil. For our struggle is not against flesh and blood [contending only with physical opponents], but against the rulers, against the powers, against the world forces of this [present] darkness, against the spiritual forces of wickedness in the heavenly (supernatural) places. Therefore, put on the complete armor of God, so that you will be able to [successfully] resist and stand your ground in the evil day [of danger], and having done everything [that the crisis demands], to stand firm [in your place, fully prepared, immovable, victorious]. So stand firm and hold your ground, HAVING TIGHTENED THE WIDE BAND OF TRUTH (personal integrity, moral courage) AROUND YOUR WAIST and HAVING PUT ON THE BREASTPLATE OF RIGHTEOUSNESS (an upright heart), and having strapped on YOUR FEET THE GOSPEL OF PEACE IN PREPARATION [to face the enemy with firm-footed stability and the readiness produced by the good news]. Above all, lift up the [protective] shield of faith with which you can extinguish all the flaming arrows of the evil one. And take

THE HELMET OF SALVATION, *and the sword of the Spirit, which is the Word of God.*

As Paul nears the end of his letter to the Ephesians, he wants to teach them one last important lesson. It is one that should be taught today; however, many avoid the subject because it could seem to be distasteful. Martyn Lloyd-Jones wrote in his book *The Christian Warfare*: "There is nothing, I would say, which is more significant about evangelicalism in the present century than the way in which it has largely ignored this teaching concerning the devil and the principalities and powers, and the 'wiles' of the devil" (D. Martyn Lloyd-Jones, *The Christian Warfare* [Grand Rapids, MI: Baker Books, 1976], 98).

We cannot defeat our enemy by sticking our heads in the sand and ignoring him. We must fully understand his strategies and deceits, and realize that God has given us what we need to protect ourselves, if we will only use it.

Paul begins this section of his letter by saying, "In conclusion, be strong in the Lord." He wants his readers to know first that we will need God's strength to enable and empower us through our union with Him. We have no power of our own to defeat the devil, but Jesus has already conquered him and given us what we need to deal with him effectively on a daily basis. Jesus came into the world for the purpose of destroying the works of the devil (1 John 3:8). He has given us victory over our enemy, and now we need to keep it.

We should always lean and rely on the Holy Spirit to help

us through our battles with the devil. Human strength alone won't suffice; we need the spiritual power that only comes from being in close, intimate relationship with the Lord. We have been given the name of Jesus, and that name has great power. Paul writes that at the mention of the name of Jesus, every knee must bow "in heaven and on earth and under the earth" (Phil. 2:10).

God has also given us armor with which to protect ourselves, and Paul instructs us to "put on the full armor of God" (Eph. 6:11). We put it on by faith, being careful to pay attention to each piece. As soldiers wearing the full armor of God, we are able to stand against the devil's lies and attacks. Paul speaks of schemes, strategies, and deceits. This lets us know that the devil has well-laid plans and is patient in his determination to deceive us.

We usually believe our struggles in life are with people or circumstances, but Paul tells us that this is not actually the case. Our struggle is not against flesh and blood; it is not against what we can see, but against unseen forces. We wrestle against evil forces that rule this world's system and are behind the present darkness we experience. This darkness manifests itself in evil of every kind, unhappiness, and lack of joy and peace. It fills the hearts of those who are deceived, and they may be unwittingly used as the devil's instrument to bring destruction.

Paul says a second time that we are to put on the complete armor of God, and when we have done so, it will enable us to stand strong in the evil day that is at hand. We are not to expect

God to do everything for us, because Paul says we should do all the crisis demands and then stand firm in our place.

Inactivity and passivity breed problems rather than solve them. We should always do what we can do and anything God instructs us to do. When we have done all we can, we have the great privilege of standing firm in Christ while we wait for the manifestation of our faith. If we do what we can do, God will always do what we cannot do. We should be ready to stand our ground and not be moved by anything we see or feel. While we are standing firm, we are to be sure we have on our armor and realize that the devil will try to take it from us.

Personal Reflection

Have you been taught to resist the deceits and strategies of the devil? Are you aware of whom your true enemy is?

_____

_____

_____

_____

_____

_____

Paul discusses six specific pieces of armor.

1. The Belt of Truth

The truth is God's Word. Anything else falls under the category of lies and deceits of the devil. Paul says to tighten the belt of truth, and that means to hang on to the Word of God during times of attack and not let anything deter us from the truth we have been taught. The literal translation of verse 14 says we are to "gird up our loins." Because the Ephesians understood this, but we may not, many modern Bible translations say to "tighten" the belt of truth.

In Paul's day, people wore tunics, cloaks, or mantles with loose ends. When people who dressed in this fashion needed to engage in vigorous activity, they had to gather the loose ends and tuck them under the waistbands (belts) of their clothing. The bands were about six inches wide and served as a type of pocket where one might carry personal items. Tucking one's clothing under the belts signified a readiness to work, compete in athletics, or prepare oneself for service or duty.

The idea of girding ourselves means we need to tighten things up, leaving no loose ends, and keep things firm. Paul is telling the Ephesians to tighten their grip on the truth (God's Word) and not let the devil steal it from them.

Attacks from the devil manifest in personal problems, and if they are long-standing or frequent, they have a wearing effect on us (Dan. 7:25). Satan seeks to wear out the saints, but God instructs us to hang on firmly to what we know He has promised. For example, if someone is trusting

God for a necessary increase in finances in their life and they unexpectedly lose their job, their first thought may be, *The things you have read in the Bible are not true, or at least they are not going to work for you.* That is the point at which they should tighten their grip on the truth and refuse to believe anything other than what God's Word says.

Personal Reflection

When trouble comes, do you keep a firm grip on the truth of God's Word, not becoming double-minded about what you believe?

_____

_____

_____

_____

_____

_____

_____

_____

2. *The Breastplate of Righteousness*

When we are under attack, the devil will insinuate that our problems are our fault and give us a generous list of all our weaknesses in the hopes of condemning us before God. This is when we must remember that through our faith in Christ, we have been made right with God. As we learned earlier in Ephesians, we are loved, accepted, and valued by God even if we make mistakes. We should live with a righteous heart, knowing we have been made right with God and are doing our utmost to walk in that righteousness. We will not hit the mark perfectly, but we can continue pressing toward the mark of perfection by not absorbing the lies of the devil.

It is important for believers in Christ to resist guilt and con-demnation, because they weaken us. Satan is the accuser of the brethren (Rev. 12:10). He accuses and assaults the conscience of God's children in an effort to make us feel we are too evil for God to love us. We cannot keep the devil from lying, because that is what he does. He lies and is the father of lies (John 8:44). It is his nature to lie, but if we will wear our armor consistently, we can protect ourselves from the devil and his lies.

When Jesus was tempted by the devil in the wilderness (Luke 4:1–13), He recognized the lies of the devil and replied, "It is written," and then He quoted Scripture. He did this repeatedly, and eventually the devil went away to wait for a more opportune time. When the devil lies to you about who you are in Christ, be prepared to talk back to him and remind him of the Word as you hold tightly to it.

Personal Reflection

How often does the devil cause you to waste time and energy feeling guilty and condemned?

_____

_____

_____

_____

_____

_____

_____

3. The Shoes of Peace

Roman soldiers wore shoes studded with a specific type of nail that gave them stability on the battlefield. Paul's reference to putting on the shoes of peace would evoke that image in the mind of his readers, but it had a great deal more significance than that.

God wants us to walk in peace. Peaceful people are powerful people. God told the Israelites when they were in battle that He would fight for them and they were to "hold [their] peace" (Exod. 14:14 NKJV). Our natural response to trouble is to become upset, but the Bible urges us to hold our peace. Remaining in peace shows that we trust God, and that is exactly what He wants us to do. The apostle Peter said we show humility by casting all our care on God (1 Pet. 5:6–7). When we worry, we use our human effort to try to solve our problems, but that never has and never will succeed. It keeps us busy, but it gets us nowhere.

Satan sets us up to get us upset, but the God we serve is wiser than he is, and He shows us what to do in every situation if we stay calm. The devil knows that if we lose our peace, we will become irrational and make emotional decisions that will only cause more trouble.

I encourage you to practice staying calm in every situation so the devil will lose his edge over you. You may remember that Paul instructs us not to let our anger last until the sun goes down, because that gives the devil an opportunity to take advantage of us (Eph. 4:26–27). We should deal with anger and any kind of upset quickly in order to protect our peace. Peace gives us power, but unbridled emotion opens a door for the devil.

Personal Reflection

Do you stay in peace in all situations? If you do lose your peace, are you able to quickly discipline your emotions and return to peace?

_____

_____

_____

_____

_____

_____

_____

_____

4. The Shield of Faith

Roman soldiers carried shields, but that armor did them no good unless they lifted it up when they needed protection. Paul doesn't say to *carry* the shield of faith, but he says to *lift it up*, and to me that means we are to use, or release, our faith in God anytime the devil attacks us in any way. Paul writes astonishing words when he says that with this shield we can extinguish all the flaming arrows of the evil one. That means we can defeat him every time he attacks if we are diligent to release the faith God has given us. We release our faith by trusting God and knowing with certainty that He is faithful. Faith prays, keeps a good confession, and is promptly obedient.

Personal Reflection

Are you lifting up your shield of faith each time the devil attacks you?

_____

_____

_____

_____

_____

_____

_____

_____

5. The Helmet of Salvation

Roman soldiers wore helmets to protect their heads in battle. We also need to wear our helmets, because we are in a spiritual war. Our helmets are not made of metal; we put them on by right thinking. I believe the helmet Paul writes about refers to making sure that our thinking is like that of a person who enjoys salvation through Jesus Christ.

We are new creations in Jesus (2 Cor. 5:17), and we are taught to think in brand-new ways. Constantly renewing the mind is one way to walk in victory, because the mind is the battlefield where the devil wages war with us. Wearing the helmet of salvation will protect us against thoughts of doubt, discouragement, and despair, as well as many other thoughts that are harmful to us.

The children of God are not protected from all trouble, but we can always have hope. Hope is a great motivator, and it keeps us moving forward in faith. Hope is available, but we must put it on. One of the most important things for us to do is to wear our helmets—meaning to choose right thinking that agrees with God's Word and His plan for our lives.

Personal Reflection

Are you careful about the kinds of thoughts you meditate on, always choosing ones that agree with God's Word?

_____

_____

_____

_____

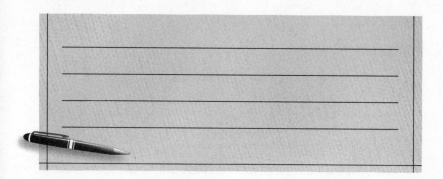

6. The Sword of the Spirit

The sword was both an offensive and a defensive weapon for the soldier. This phrase "the sword of the Spirit" is used only once in the Bible, here in Ephesians. Paul wants us to realize that we have God's Word as both an offensive weapon and a defensive one. Each child of God is engaged in a battle with evil spiritual forces, and one of the best ways to defeat them is to attack them with God's Word. Meditate on it, believe it, speak it, fill your prayers with it, and obey it.

I have found speaking God's Word aloud to be especially helpful to me, and many others have experienced the same thing. I urge you to form a habit of speaking God's Word regularly, especially when you feel the devil is attacking you in any way. For example, if you start to feel discouraged, you can say, "The joy of the Lord is my strength, and He is on my side, always fighting for me." Or, if you feel that you don't have the strength or energy to finish a commitment or task that needs to be done, you can say, "God is my strength, and He enables me to do all things through Christ."

Personal Reflection

Are you using your sword of the Spirit, which is the Word of God, to help you defeat the devil and aid you in keeping your mind renewed?

_____

_____

_____

_____

_____

_____

_____

_____

The six pieces of armor Paul introduces are extremely valuable, but we must always remember that they don't help us unless we put them on and use them. We wouldn't go out of our houses naked or half-dressed, and neither should we go about daily life without putting on the armor of God.

Cover Everything with Prayer

Ephesians 6:18–24

With all prayer and petition pray [with specific requests]
at all times [on every occasion and in every season] in the
Spirit, and with this in view, stay alert with all perseverance
and petition [interceding in prayer] for all God's people.
And pray for me, that words may be given to me when
I open my mouth, to proclaim boldly the mystery of the
good news [of salvation], for which I am an ambassador
in chains. And pray that in proclaiming it I may speak
boldly and courageously, as I should. Now, so that you
may know how I am and what I am doing, Tychicus, the
beloved brother and faithful minister in the Lord, will tell
you everything. I have sent him to you for this very purpose,
so that you may know how we are, and that he may comfort
and encourage and strengthen your hearts. Peace be to the
brothers and sisters, and love joined with faith, from God
the Father and the Lord Jesus Christ. Grace be with all who
love our Lord Jesus Christ with undying and incorruptible
love.

Now Paul says we are to cover everything with prayer, praying at all times about all things. The privilege of prayer is one
of the greatest gifts God has given us, and we should be alert

at all times to open the door for God's help through praying. God is interested in every aspect of our lives and wants to help us with all the things that concern us. We need to cover our homes, children, marriages, finances, minds, health—anything we want to be protected—with prayer.

Praying about all things at all times is one way to develop an intimate relationship with the Lord. Not only is He interested in your spiritual life, but He wants to be part of all that you do, so be diligent to invite Him to help you constantly by covering everything with prayer. This is simple to do, but very powerful and effective.

Paul also asks the Ephesians to remember to pray for him, especially that God would give him the right words when he opened his mouth to teach and preach, and that he would always boldly proclaim the gospel.

Paul closes this letter to the Ephesians by speaking peace and grace to them. It is obvious from Paul's language that with all of his heart he wants God's people to remain firm in their faith and to enjoy the life that Jesus provided for them through His death and resurrection.

Paul is also speaking to us today through this letter, and I pray that you will read and study it over and over and continue to benefit from it.

Personal Reflection

Are you standing firm in your faith, praying at all times about everything that concerns you, and enjoying the life Jesus died to give you?

_____

_____

_____

_____

_____

_____

_____

_____

_____

_____

_____

_____

_____

_____

_____

_____

Do you have a real relationship with Jesus?

God loves you! He created you to be a special, unique, one-of-a-kind individual, and He has a specific purpose and plan for your life. And through a personal relationship with your Creator—God—you can discover a way of life that will truly satisfy your soul.

No matter who you are, what you've done, or where you are in your life right now, God's love and grace are greater than your sin—your mistakes. Jesus willingly gave His life so you can receive forgiveness from God and have new life in Him. He's just waiting for you to invite Him to be your Savior and Lord.

If you are ready to commit your life to Jesus and follow Him, all you have to do is ask Him to forgive your sins and give you a fresh start in the life you are meant to live. Begin by praying this prayer...

Lord Jesus, thank You for giving Your life for me and forgiving me of my sins so I can have a personal relationship with You. I am sincerely sorry for the mistakes I've made, and I know I need You to help me live right.

Your Word says in Romans 10:9, "If you declare with your mouth, 'Jesus is Lord,' and believe in your heart that God raised him from the dead, you will be saved" (NIV). I believe You are the Son of God and confess You as my Savior and Lord. Take me just as I am, and work in my heart, making me the person You want me to be. I want to live for You, Jesus, and I am so grateful that You are giving me a fresh start in my new life with You today.

I love You, Jesus!

It's so amazing to know that God loves us so much! He wants to have a deep, intimate relationship with us that grows every day as we spend time with Him in prayer and Bible study. And we want to encourage you in your new life in Christ.

Please visit joycemeyer.org/knowJesus to request Joyce's book *A New Way of Living*, which is our gift to you. We also have other free resources online to help you make progress in pursuing everything God has for you.

Congratulations on your fresh start in your life in Christ! We hope to hear from you soon.

ABOUT THE AUTHOR

JOYCE MEYER is one of the world's leading practical Bible teachers. A *New York Times* bestselling author, Joyce's books have helped millions of people find hope and restoration through Jesus Christ. Joyce's programs, *Enjoying Everyday Life* and *Everyday Answers with Joyce Meyer*, air around the world on television, radio, and the Internet. Through Joyce Meyer Ministries, Joyce teaches internationally on a number of topics with a particular focus on how the Word of God applies to our everyday lives. Her candid communication style allows her to share openly and practically about her experiences so others can apply what she has learned to their lives.

Joyce has authored more than one hundred books, which have been translated into more than one hundred languages, and over 65 million of her books have been distributed worldwide. Bestsellers include *Power Thoughts*; *The Confident Woman*; *Look Great, Feel Great*; *Starting Your Day Right*; *Ending Your Day Right*; *Approval Addiction*; *How to Hear from God*; *Beauty for Ashes*; and *Battlefield of the Mind*.

Joyce's passion to help hurting people is foundational to

the vision of Hand of Hope, the missions arm of Joyce Meyer Ministries. Hand of Hope provides worldwide humanitarian outreaches such as feeding programs, medical care, orphanages, disaster response, human trafficking intervention and rehabilitation, and much more—always sharing the love and gospel of Christ.

JOYCE MEYER MINISTRIES

U.S. AND FOREIGN OFFICE ADDRESSES

Joyce Meyer Ministries
P.O. Box 655
Fenton, MO 63026
USA
(636) 349-0303

Joyce Meyer Ministries—Canada
P.O. Box 7700
Vancouver, BC V6B 4E2
Canada
(800) 868-1002

Joyce Meyer Ministries—Australia
Locked Bag 77
Mansfield Delivery Centre
Queensland 4122
Australia
(07) 3349 1200

Joyce Meyer Ministries—England
P.O. Box 1549
Windsor SL4 1GT
United Kingdom
01753 831102

Joyce Meyer Ministries—South Africa
P.O. Box 5
Cape Town 8000
South Africa
(27) 21-701-1056

Other Books by Joyce Meyer

The Power of Being Thankful

The Power of Determination

The Power of Forgiveness

The Power of Simple Prayer

Power Thoughts

Power Thoughts Devotional

Reduce Me to Love

The Secret Power of Speaking God's Word

The Secrets of Spiritual Power

The Secret to True Happiness

Seize the Day*

Seven Things That Steal Your Joy

Starting Your Day Right

Start Your New Life Today

Straight Talk

Teenagers Are People Too!

Trusting God Day by Day

The Word, the Name, the Blood

Unshakeable Trust*

Woman to Woman

You Can Begin Again

Your Battles Belong to the Lord*

Joyce Meyer Spanish Titles

20 Maneras de Hacer Que Cada Día Sea Major (20 Ways to
Make Every Day Better)

Aproveche Su Día (Seize the Day)

* Study guide available for this title

Books by Dave Meyer

Life Lines